CHARLESTOWN
Built on Lime

Norman Fotheringham

Published by Charlestown Lime Heritage Trust, November, 1997.
Reprinted June, 2010

ISBN 0 947559 55 8

Note:- *Imperial units are used throughout this account – there is a conversion table in the appendix.*

Front Cover:- *"Extensive Kilns and Rail Network at Charlestown".*

CONTENTS

FOREWORD BY EARL OF ELGIN

 Ever since the industrial development of Culross from the middle of the 16th century the Bruce Family has continued to buy land for commercial and agricultural development. On the Gellet lands south of Dunfermline there was a huge outcrop of limestone which,, if quarried, reduced in size and burned with coal would provide excellent material for the building trade to bond their ashlar and bricks. The farmer also would hugely benefit his land from the application of burned lime and other trades and crafts also were in the way for specialist reasons, iron foundries, glass makers, distillers and brewers. None of this would be practical without men to quarry and carts and sailors to transport by land and sea and fortunately, the lime crags were hard by the river shore. The moving spirit was Charles, 5th Earl of Elgin returning from the Grand Tour of Europe in 1756 and, in an incredibly short space of time, he overcame practical difficulties and the operation began in 1759. Lord Elgin's mother gravely disapproved of the enterprise which required the building of houses for at least one hundred and fifty families, a small harbour, several large lime kilns and a wagon road for coal.

For a century and a half this unit of the enlightened age worked. Sheer size perhaps gave it economy of scale which, in turn, allowed a sharp price structure to beat off competitors but eventually the quarry material was worked out and more modern methods of reducing lime to a suitable size took over in the commercial scene. Bit by bit the hive of activity regressed but people stayed on content to live in historic company with the sweat, grime and success of yesteryears.

I commend the detailed account of Lord Elgin's Works which has been compiled by Norman Fotheringham.

Elgin.

AUTHOR'S NOTE

I would like to acknowledge the assistance and encouragement provided by the Earl of Elgin and Kincardine. His family of Bruce have been the landowners in this area for around three centuries and this whole fascinating story is largely due to this continuous ownership. Lord Elgin is a fountain of knowledge on our local history and much of the material has come directly from him and his extensive archives at Broomhall. Thanks are also due to the laird for his many additions to the text and for correcting my many mistakes with his blue pencil.

CHARLESTOWN .... BUILT ON LIME

INTRODUCTION

This story, for long dormant and waiting to be told, is one of great initiative, carried out by one man, Charles 5th Earl of Elgin. It begins in mid 18th century - just after the '45 rising, when the Jacobites, including Earl Charles' mother Lady Kincardine, were still hiding in the bushes. Large landowners were thinking of what to do with their land and most turned to farming. Charles did not then own a great deal of land in West Fife but his estate had an enormous seam of accessible limestone which could be easily worked and put to use.

This was the beginning of the industrial revolution in Scotland and we could claim Charlestown to be the birthplace of organised work on any scale... the very earliest integrated work complex in the land, conceived in 1752 and functional within a decade. Limestone was the basis of much of the country's future... used mainly for building purposes, for sweetening the soil in agriculture and as a flux in such activities as iron and glass making.

This is a tale of how, using local materials, Charles built a small self-sufficient town - Charles' town - in the shape of his initials CE. In a very short time there grew the village, by far the largest range of kilns in the country, a harbour, sutlery, school and all of the essential elements of the planned village.

As the story unfolds, the reader will be taken back 2 ½ centuries to the sounds of chisels cutting sandstone, blasting in the quarries and the bell summoning the workers to the day's labour. Barefooted children wander to school past the blacksmith's shop where the Smith is busy at his trade with 50 pairs of horse stabled nearby. There is the strong aroma of sulphur and ammonia which permeates the air from the limeburning. Horse-drawn carts creak and rumble along the wooden wagonways as the carters urge their charges with the day's loads. Busy ladies are bleaching blankets on the laundry green well away from the cloud of smoke carried by the prevailing wind from the kilns. In the evening the glow from the fires may be seen for miles around and the sounds of foreign tongues can be heard from the inn, showing the international connections of the place.

We shall discuss the main elements in turn - the kilns, the quarries, the harbour, the village, the granary with the sutlery, the Elgin railway, the school, the laundry and also the peripherals - not forgetting the most important ingredient of all, the people and characters who lived here and made it all possible and who thought that this enterprise in a tiny corner of the Kingdom of Fife, created by Charles and which satisfied a large part of Scotland's need for lime and from where exports went to much of Europe and further, was indeed the centre of the universe.

CHAPTER ONE

THE PLAN

The concept of the PLANNED VILLAGE came to Scotland in the 18th century. Prior to this, settlements were not organised in any way : there was no social or aesthetic motivation nor was it part of any scheme to aid the development of the estate or encourage economic growth of the country. The idea was to change all of this and to contrive a new framework for the life of the people.

Most landowners turned to agriculture and the first change was to alter the old runrig methods of farming. The disappearance of this meant the emergence of capitalist farmers. Fewer people were working on the farms but bigger crops were cultivated. Lord Elgin did not at this time have a great deal of land in West Fife but there was an enormous seam of limestone on his estate. The processing of this was to give an alternative source of employment and lead to the creation of the village.

Primarily the planned village was required to house the families of the workers but it also had to be a place of employment for those made redundant from the changes in farming. This was most serious in the North with the Highland Clearances and it is probable that Charlestown was able to attract some workers from this source. In the 1790's advertisements were placed in the Nothern News. We have an area of the village called Lochaber and there are still a lot of McDonalds about the place! Landowners were conscious of their social obligations and the problems that land clearances were causing. There was a lot of emigration, but the formation of the villages created a measure of stability and the opportunity of new employment. This was the beginning of the industrial revolution in Scotland.

The ideas were of course circulating amongst the lairds. Some plans were imported from England after the '45. So we had works, schools, shops, post-offices and even prisons. It is always difficult to know where a plan or idea came from. Probably this had been at the back of Charles' mind for some time. Perhaps it came from Rome! Actually Earl Charles and Robert Adam met in Rome in 1756. Adam was then a young architect of 25. They met at a St Andrew's Day party at which Adam wrote later that he became "unco fu" and Lord Elgin sang droll Scots songs. Perhaps the plan crystallised in Charles' mind at this meeting. We shall never know.

This period has also been referred to as the "age of enlightenment" in Scotland. There was the philosophy of Robert Owen who came to David Dale's New Lanark in 1799. This set out the concepts of social justice for all, the dignity of the workers, and the village being a self-contained community providing education and social amenities as well as employment. Charlestown was well established before this time. Charles' plan dates from 1752 and the buildings started in 1756. However, there is no doubt that this ideal was attempted by

South Row, Charlestown

Charles, and later by Thomas, in Charlestown. This then was the theory - how did it work in practice?

It has been calculated that there were over 100 model villages planned in Scotland. Some like Charlestown, were completely new, whilst others were attempts to reconstruct existing settlements. There were groups around the Clyde, in the Lothians, in Angus., Banff and Moray. Only one, Charlestown, was in Fife.

The architectural plan was always simple with the houses arranged in rows. Charlestown was laid out in the shape of the founder's initials CE, with around a hundred houses. One interesting feature of most plans was the absence of a front garden. This has puzzled many folks today and it has caused a lot of problems. It had been the extremely unhealthy practice to have a dunghill with all the filth outside the front door. This midden could be prevented by having the door open directly onto the pavement. In Charlestown a fair proportion of the dwellings front straight onto the road, but there was another method of dealing with sewage, to be discussed later.

Most lairds were dictators and believed in absolute power. The control of the inhabitants was generally in the hands of the factor c.f. Thomas's rules of 1815. Those would naturally not be tolerated today, but were necessary at the time to provide structure and organisation for the benefit of all.

Of the many varieties of planned village, Charlestown may probably be classified as a factory/industrial type. Without question it was successful, and I believe unique.

Generally the movement to planned villages in the land can properly be described as a big failure. In the Highlands we were left with a set of crofters' huts and in the Lowlands the concept was killed by the onset of railways and large industrial activities. Some grew into towns - Callander, Crieff, Ballater, Fort Augustus, Inveraray, Kingussie and Ullapool being amongst them. Most however lost the plan and character as originally envisaged. There were few exceptions. The well known New Lanark reached maturity but Charlestown developed to probably achieve the lofty aims of its creator.

For a community of 100 houses and around 500 inhabitants, the place has in its precincts a school, granary, sutlery, blacksmith's shop, estate workshops, village hall, laundry, bakery, dairy, inn, saltworks, sawmill, the most extensive set of kilns in Europe, a large harbour, extensive rail network with passenger station, an iron foundry, 6 mills on the Lyne Burn, stables and brickworks. The whole is surrounded by Broomhall Estate with its farms and "big house". There were lime, sandstone and whin quarries.

We shall look at each of those components in turn in more detail, but where in Scotland is there another such place?

Clearly we are dealing with something quite unique in this tiny spot. The importance of Charlestown is evident from the survival of the place as originally planned two and a half centuries ago. Nowhere else in the land can the relationship between the community and the elements of places of work be so clearly seen.

THE ELGINS OF BROOMHALL

The seat at Broomhall was completed in 1704 with later additions by the 7th Earl reflecting his classical tastes. This mansion stands proudly high above the village of Limekilns, in extensive grounds and has been the home of the Earls and their families since then. Inside the mansion is a collection of objects of art from many lands brought back by a succession of illustrious Lairds. There is the two-handed sword of Robert the Bruce and it is appropriate this should be in the possession of the Chief of the Bruce family. The sword had been for long kept in Clackmannan Tower and, on the complete demise of the Bruces of Clackmannan, the sword and other items were bequeathed to the 7th Earl in 1796.

The family bought part of the Estate in 1588 and gradually gained more over the years - the rest of Limekilns coming in 1815. The first Bruce at Broomhall Estate was Robert Bruce of Blairhall and later Sir Alexander Bruce of Broomhall became the 4th Earl of Kincardine in 1705. Three of his sons were to succeed to the title. The youngest of those (7th Earl of Kincardine) alone left an heir. The founder of the village, Charles was his grandson. He also inherited the Elgin title and so the titles merged as 5th Earl of Elgin and 9th of Kincardine and it is with this gentleman that the Charlestown story begins.

Earl Charles died in 1771 and his oldest son William died later in the same year and so the titles came to Thomas the illustrious 7th Earl of Elgin (1766-1841). He was a distinguished ambassador to the Turkish Empire and is best remembered for rescuing the Elgin Marbles, which were in danger of being destroyed, from the Acropolis and Parthenon in Greece. This operation cost him a fortune and he disposed of them to the British Museum in 1816 for far less than his costs. He was labelled by some as a vandal for his pains. There are still arguments today over this acquisition but it is clear that surely those treasures would have been lost to us otherwise.

Public service had become the order and 8th Earl James was Ambassador/Governor to China, India, Jamaica and Canada. He acted as Postmaster General in the Government and died whilst on duty as Viceroy in 1863.

The next Earl was Victor Alexander. In 1890 Fife County Council was set up with the Earl as its first Chairman. He was given the freedom of Dunfermline in 1893 and was appointed Viceroy & Governor-General of India in the same year. He held this post until 1897. His sister Lady Louisa Bruce had unveiled the brass in the floor of Dunfermline Abbey above the tomb of Robert the Bruce. The Earl later served as Secretary of State for the Colonies.

The 10th Earl succeeded his father in 1917. There were many royal visits to the area and Broomhall. In 1923 King George V and Queen Mary became the first reigning monarchs to visit the area for 300 years. Also attending were the Duke of York (King George VI) and the Duchess (Queen Mother). The King and the Queen passed through the villages and a splendid guard of honour of girl-guides, led by my Aunt Ella, was lined up outside the pierhead school.

Visits to Broomhall continued. The Duke of Windsor (later Edward VIII) stayed there in 1933 and the Duke and Duchess of York later in same year. There was an informal visit by Queen Mary in 1938. The Earl received the freedom of the Burgh in 1938. George VI and Queen Elizabeth visited the area in 1945 in March and later in September. They also were here in 1948. I recall being caught unawares by the famous smile and, wave of the Queen Mother as she passed unexpectedly through the village in 1955 on her way from Broomhall to Culross. There stands the other mansion of the Estate. The Earl "retired" there and became Provost of Culross.

The present Earl is the 11th of Elgin and 15th of Kincardine. He has carried on the family tradition of public service and being involved in national activities. What is important to the people of Charlestown is that he has succeeded in preserving, almost intact, this small corner as a place of which we are all very conscious that we live in a unique spot. The eldest son, Lord Bruce, is appropriately another Charles. He is currently acting as Estate factor planning for the future of Charles' town. The survival of the place in its original form is due entirely to the fact that the Estate has been in the ownership of this family for around 300 years.

Thomas, 7th Earl of Elgin, in uniform of Scots Guards

CHAPTER TWO

THE LIME TRAIL

LIME

Charlestown is founded on lime and so it is appropriate that we investigate just what the stuff is, without becoming too technical. Basically limestone is calcium carbonate (chalk) which exists in many forms - in Charlestown it is coral, which was laid down over 300 million years ago, and is full of fossils. Even in those far off days the Scottish weather produced a harder substance than in England, where softer limestone and chalk abound. In Charlestown the stone had to be quarried out and this became progressively more difficult as the seam ran downwards.

THE PROCESS:-

At the works, the limestone is heated - coal being the fuel - to a very high temperature of around 900C, and the result is quicklime (calcium oxide), referred to at the works as lime shell. In appearance it looks rather like the clinkers left from a coal fire, and is much lighter than the original stone with around 40% weight loss during the burning.

The second stage is the SLAKING process. Quicklime is highly caustic and must be handled carefully. It produces a violent reaction with water. This is spectacular since the temperature shoots up and the mixture boils whilst turning white. The product is calcium hydroxide - lime - putty or builder lime. Finally this mortar, when- it is used for building, will over a period dry out slowly and return to chalk. There are of course variations of this and different skills are required to give the desired result. Those chemical and physical changes are often referred to as the LIME CYCLE.

1)   heat

$CaCO_3 \longrightarrow CaO + CO_2$ BURNING

Limestone   Quicklime Carbon Dioxide

2)

$CaO + H_2O \longrightarrow Ca(OH)_2 + heat$ SLAKING

Calcium Oxide Water   Calcium Hydroxide

3)

$Ca(OH)_2 + CO_2$ —time $\longrightarrow CaCO_3 + H_2O$ BUILDING

Hydrated lime Carbon Dioxide Calcium Carbonate Dries out

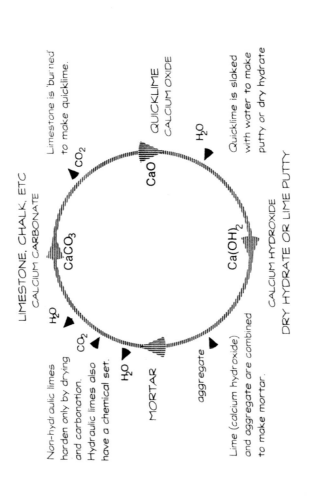

LIMESTONE, CHALK, ETC
CALCIUM CARBONATE

Limestone is 'burned'
to make quicklime.

CO_2

QUICKLIME
CALCIUM OXIDE

$CaCO_3$

CaO

H_2O

Quicklime is slaked
with water to make
putty or dry hydrate

H_2O

CO_2

$Ca(OH)_2$

Non-hydraulic limes
harden only by drying
and carbonation.
Hydraulic limes also
have a chemical set.

H_2O

CALCIUM HYDROXIDE
DRY HYDRATE OR LIME PUTTY

MORTAR

aggregate

Lime (calcium hydroxide)
and aggregate are combined
to make mortar.

SIMPLIFIED DIAGRAM OF THE LIME CYCLE

In Charlestown stage 1 was carried out at the limeworks in the kilns and quicklime produced. Stage 2 was also done on site with the production of slaked lime or powdered lime. This stage however was frequently carried out at the quicklime's destination. This meant that the dangerous load had to be transported, almost entirely by ship. Stage 3 is the usage of the product for building purposes or in agriculture. In the latter, crushed shells could just be scattered on the ground leaving nature to perform the other 2 stages and so improve the fertility of the soil.

The properties of lime have been known for thousands of years, though not perhaps the chemical reactions just described. It has played a vital part in the industrial development of the country. The obvious uses are in building and agriculture but lime was, and still is, used as a flux in such manufactures as iron, soap and glass.

It is worth looking in more detail at the use of lime in building. Prior to the arrival of cement, stone buildings were constructed using lime mortars. In Scotland the exterior of the building was protected by a cover of lime mortar, perhaps ½ to 1" thick. Frequently the finishing coat was a lime wash of a pretty colour e.g. yellow, white, pink or green. This was certainly more attractive than the cement harlings common today.

Many old historic buildings have over the years been incorrectly repaired using cement. This does not have the same properties as lime which will allow the building to breathe. THE SCOTTISH LIME CENTRE has recently been established in the village with the objective of correcting this situation. Perhaps there will be a revival in the usage of lime as it is intended to build a kiln and produce lime again at Charlestown.

TECHNICAL NOTE

The quarries at Charlestown extend for about a mile. The original "Glen Hole" quarry is full of water but West Quarry can be investigated. The thickness of the seam varies between 6ft and 60ft. The overburden on the face shows approx clay 10ft deep and shale/blaes of 30ft. Then there is 10ft of poor quality limestone and then the main seam of 25ft. This seam is good quality and contains much shell and crinoids. The stone shows calcium carbonate CACO, around 70% and magnesium carbonate $MgCO_3$ of approx 30%.

THE LIME TRAIL

This commences in the quarries, runs down the wagonways and tramways to the limeworks, through the kilns, onto ships and perhaps finishes up with some farmers along the River Tay.

THE QUARRIES

For many years limestone had been dug above the village of Limekilns. The stones were rolled down to the beach to be burned in primitive kilns. When Earl Charles came along, he organised all of this. To begin with the stone was near the surface and was worked directly downwards. The middle quarry is now a lake. This quarry began to fill with water and, though a stationary steam engine was introduced to pump it out, the water won and the quarry moved westward. The GELLET ROCK was left as a monument to mark the original height of the surface. This is a 60ft cube of limestone crowned by a flagpole with intricate rigging. It contains many fossils and was left to remind posterity of the prodigious nature of the early quarrying work. It stands high above the villages and is quite a landmark.

Limestone Quarry at Charlestown

The method of reaching the seam of limestone was by "tirring". This was the removal of the overburden, usually blaes. In some of this work BLONDINS were used to disperse the unwanted materials. This was an overhead set of cables on which baskets were suspended. (c.f. the tightrope walker Blondini who walked across the Niagara falls blindfold with his feet in baskets). To the North of Charlestown we have large mounds of the stuff abandoned by the quarriers and now covered with trees making a fine backdrop.

As the work moved West, the lime strata ran deeper and this method of mining had to be replaced. The search went into caves or adits. Those are around 30ft high, the depth of the seam, and separated by 10ft wide limestone pillars. Those are very spectacular and it is hoped to make one or two suitable for public viewing.

The quarries extend for around 1 mile East to West and are ½ mile wide. It has been calculated that over the two centuries that lime was mined here, more than 11 million tons were quarried. The slopes behind the village have been lowered by quite a few metres.

The method of mining was firstly to remove the topsoil etc. A hole was drilled into the stone by a two man team. One man held the jumper chisel and the other hit it with a large sledgehammer. The drill could be driven 6ft into the rock. This was very hard work - and dangerous for the one holding the chisel! GUNPOWDER was then used to blast out the stone. This was dangerous also but accidents decreased when improved powder and realiable fuses were introduced in the early 19th century. Gunpowder had to be brought from England and was a major expense in the operation, until powder was made in Scotland.

Quarrying Limestone

At this time, as was common in Scotland, the quarriers worked in squads of 6 men. There were six or seven squads in the mines. They worked a sort of piecework system and the payment was determined by the amount of stone delivered. This might seem an enlightened scheme with payment by results. However there were big drawbacks for the worker, the employer and the customer. Each squad was allocated an area for the season and on this an estimate was made of how much would be extracted. A bargain was struck and from this a sort of credit system, which allowed for goods and rent to be drawn in advance operated. A pay bill of 1814 shows that a squad could earn around 7 or 8d (3p) per ton of limestone. There was a deduction for the quantity of gunpowder used so that 2000 tons would give about £50. This rarely was enough to cover the amount owed over the period and so the workers went into constant debt to the Estate. Quarriers also had no control of the weather or the demand for lime.

Gellet Rock

Limework Pay Bill for April, paid 11th May 1814

	Tons	Sometime Rate Amount	Deduction Gunpowder &c by Amount	Balance
Carrying William McLeish & Company	1919	6/7¾ £57 6 ..	300 15 ..	£42 6 ..
Henry Aubrics Company	1595	69¼ 65 7 ..	100 20 ..	15 7 ..
David Blyth & Company	1804	0.. 65 14 4½	450 22 10	43 4 4
Robert Watts & Company	2920	6/7¼ 89 4 5	400 20	69 4 5
	3038	£277 11 10	1850 77 10	£200 1 10

Received from the Earl of Elgin by the hands of Andrew Thomson the above Balance of
Two hundred and one pounds ten .. /10/ —

Gavin Blyth
Henry Aubrics
John McLeman
Robert Watts

The Estate factor in 1805 was W. Wotherspoon and the General Manager was Charles Landale, a civil engineer. The factor always had a great deal of power in running the Estate. The Earls were frequently abroad and the day to day management was delegated. Landale decided that the system was not efficient and changed it. Once the quarriers had gone into debt and could see no way out of it, they became resigned to their fate, and production fell. Landale wrote off all of the accumulated debt and his new system led to the quarriers making more money than he had intended. He made other improvements which kept the kilnhead men and the quarry people busy during the winter months. They were employed in tirring in preparation and also stocks of limestone were built up at the works. Landale also tightened up the credit system and bills had to be settled sooner.

By the 1930's the lime caves of the West Quarry were filling rapidly with water. Quarrying was still going on under what is now the cricket pitch, but the roof kept collapsing and it was decided to abandon quarrying in 1937. Incidentally ½ a century later, Broomhall Cricket Club have had big problems in getting good grass to grow on the square, which is on top of a lime pit. The limeworks however continued to operate on a reduced scale with limestone brought in until 1956.

WAGONWAYS AND TRAMWAYS

The limestone had to be delivered to the works. Fortunately this was a distance of only about ½ mile. From the original East and Mid Quarries this was done by horsedrawn carts. The routes changed as the quarries moved westward, but they all finished up at the entrance to the kilnhead. This is alongside the Run and so this was a busy area with coal and limestone being delivered, and wagonways fanning out. From the Middle quarry those ran through the village which was not then completed. North Row was the last to be built, partly because of this traffic. In the summer, when quarrying was at its peak, the roads were busy with carters and their loads. In the season 50 extra pairs of horse came over from the Bo'ness area. The carters and the horses had to be accommodated and the stables were in Stable Row (now Rocks Road) opposite the school.

Around 100,000 tons were being extracted per year and, since this was only done in the better weather months, this was probably 5000 tons per week or something like 1000 tons a day. The early wagons held perhaps 2 tons and so there were many return journeys per day.

This slow and painful journey was replaced by the construction of the TUNNEL. This is how the locals refer to the rail link built from the mines to the kilnhead. This tramway carried stone from the West quarry. There was a stationary steam engine at the GINHEAD and this was used to pull up loaded trucks which then descended to the kilns through a tunnel. Much of this route survives and can be seen. The engine house and base for the steam engine are there. The BRIDGE over West Road had 2 arches. One for the Elgin Railway and the other for road traffic. It had to be knocked down in 1935 since double-decker buses could not get through, but the abutments are still there on either side of the road. The cutting and tunnel beside the Elgin Hotel are still evident. This plateway is deemed to be of historic importance and is a scheduled monument. It is, however, unlikely that it could be restored; for one thing it runs between the gardens of private houses!

Train at the Kilns

CHARLESTOWN
(Firth of Forth)

LIMEWORKS,

❋

· Lime despatched by Sea or Rail ·

THE WORKS

The limeworks are a massive structure completely dominating the harbour and surrounding area. In their day they were the largest lime producing complex in Europe and supplied $1/3$ of Scotland's total production. Considering that they worked hard for 2 centuries, and the nature of the work, it is surprising that they survive today in what is remarkably good condition. This is of course an A-listed scheduled monument.

Earl Charles originally built 6 kilns; those were later increased to 14. They are built into the side of a bank or cliff and form one large continuous building with each kiln connected to its neighbours by cathedral-like passages.

There were many types of kiln in existence, from the primitive clamp type made of turf to the high-tech modern ones of today. Charlestown's are all of the same type of construction, though some are larger than others. The original 6 held 200 tons, whereas nos 13 and 14 held 500 tons. They are basically all 30ft high vertical cylinders open at the top with 4 drawholes or eyelets at the base. The drawholes are all under cover and in the first 6 the workers could actually operate under the kiln. The drawholes had iron doors (there is still one which has survived intact) which could regulate the flow of air into the chamber and so govern the rate of burning. This could be done to meet the current demand for lime and ensure a good burn. It also meant that the quicklime drawn out could be partly cooled so that the barrows were not set fire to, nor the drawers quite so uncomfortable. Those eyelets were around 3ft above the ground at a convenient height to allow the shells to be raked out.

THE KILNHEAD

Because of the location of the kilns against a high bank, the plateau of the kilnhead was extensive. Coal would be delivered straight there without having to be hoisted up. There was room for all of the activities as well as piles of stone and coal. Unfortunately none of the buildings on the top has survived. They were demolished after the works closed in 1956 and the equipment sold. The easiest way to get rid of the debris from this clearance was to tip it in to the nearby kilns. Only no 14 remains completely empty though it would be fairly easy to clear some of the others. There is photographic evidence of the buildings which included a slaking house, engineer's shed, storage and a crusher house.

METHODS

This was really quite unsophistocated. The kilnheadmen tipped from a barrow, thick layers of coal and limestone into the open shaft. The burning was continuous and, once going, each kiln was topped up from time to time. The glow from the fires must have been a splendid sight for miles around, especially from over the river. It could take up to a fortnight for a piece of stone to journey from top to bottom. Lime shell was drawn from the eyes into small carts. Much of this could go straight into ships for onward sales. There was a narrow gauge internal rail system so that loads of quicklime could be pulled by a rope back up to the top. Here it was either powdered or slaked. This was simple and straightforward but of course there were problems.

The design of the kilns meant that a lot of heat was lost via the open top and was one of the reasons that the kilnhead men applied too much coal. The lining of the kilns required to be repaired with firebricks every 2 or 3 years and naturally the kiln had to be closed down for this. The heat level is critical to the quality of the final product and this was difficult to control. Often stone was unburned giving rise to complaints from the customers. The demand for quicklime was not steady and it was difficult to store. Often the shells were left in the kilns too long if the demand was slow and the reverse if high.

Another fault of the system was that payment of the workforce was for quantity and not quality. The optimum size of stone was around the size of a man's fist. The quarriers would deliver large chunks and these should have been broken down using a sledgehammer. Charlestown stone was very hard and this was a difficult task. If the overseer was not around, the large bits would go in. This was always a constant battle with the workers. The largest pieces of stone went in the middle and the smaller round the outside. This constant friction was always there and the kilnhead men were stubborn and reluctant to change their ways.

The ratio of coal to limestone is difficult to pinpoint. This depended on many factors - the quality of the coal, the hardness of the stone and the feelings and disposition of the workers. Since the workers did not pay for the coal, it is likely that more than was necessary was used. However in a draw kiln such as Charlestown's, a ratio of between 1 to 5 and 1 to 10 would be the recipe. Taking the weight loss of the lime in the kiln into account, it is likely that 1 ton of coal and from 5 to 10 tons of stone at the kilnhead, would produce from 3 to 6 tons of quicklime at the exit. Clearly there are many variables in this, not least the skill of the operators.

The efficient burning could be determined by various clues. One was the type of smoke coming out. In Charlestown this was complicated by the impurities in the stone. Heavy smoke means that more air is needed. Flames emerging means that lime must be drawn out and the draught regulated. A light haze would indicate good burning. Clear air coming out indicates that there is too much draught. The weather was another factor and heavy rain was not good news.

SLAKING

Quicklime will over a period of time, depending on the humidity, combine with water vapour in the air. This is fine if it is in a building as lime mortar, but will spoil fresh quicklime which is therefore difficult to store. It was desirable to get the lime shells to their destination as quickly as possible.

At the limeworks, shells which were not for immediate sale were slaked. This would give lime putty which is a fine building material and easily stored over a period. Alternatively by adding less water in the slaking process, dry hydrate of lime would be the result. This powdered lime is light and easily stored and transported. This would be the preferred product at Charlestown and could be sent and changed into putty and building mortar on site.

On the kilnhead there was a slaking shed and large tanks. The shells were originally broken down by hand and later by a mechanical crusher. This was then spread in the bath. Water is added and the mixture stirred with a wooden rake. The temperature would rise and the water bubble as slaking takes place. This occurs around 1000C and stirring should continue until slaking has stopped. There were settlement tanks so that the liquid could flow into them and settle. More shells could be added to the slaking tank.

Of the lime products at Charlestown, generally the agricultural folks would take quicklime shells and use them on their farms. For building purposes, the product was usually powdered lime converted to mortar by the builders.

Limeworkers at Kilnhead

THE WORKERS

At the works there were men employed as kilnheadmen, drawers, trimmers, slakers and emptiers. Those were all paid by results, and as previously explained, this did not always work to the advantage of any of the parties. A wagebill of 1814 shows the payment of limestone workers and shippers:-

At this time a variety of Scots measures were used. Most of those were by volume and not weight, and also varied according to the locality or what was being measured. Consequently it is difficult to be precise about the quantities involved or their conversions to weights.

Lime was produced in bolls (or bowls or bolles). This was a measure of 6 bushels (1 bushel - 8 gallons) and weighed around 1 ¼ cwts. Slaked lime was made in chalders and this was 16 bolls or about 20 cwts (1 ton) for lime and 25 ½ cwts for coal. Although this may be imprecise and confusing, it only applied to the kiln workers. Quarrying was measured in tons and coal and lime were sold and shipped in tons (see the trade). So we can be confident from the Estate records of the amounts quarried and sold on.

Kilnheadmen	5/9 (27p)	per 100 bolls	loading kilns
Drawers	3/3 (16p)	per 100 bolls	raking our shells
Trimmers	1/4 (6p)	per 100 bolls	shipped loading
Slakers	1/2 (6p)	per chalder	made and shipped
Emptiers	11/6 (57p)	per 100 wagons of 3 tons each	

For shipping limestone:

11/6 (57p)	per 100 tons shipped

Sawyers for sawing hardwood	4/6 (22p)	per 100 ft (30m)
Sawyers for sawing fir	2/6 (12p)	per 100 ft (30m)

This document also lists wages for Masons, Wrights, Labourers and Overseers.

At this time altogether in the works, there were about 200 men employed and the annual production was around 1,400,000 bolls or 90,000 tons of lime.

Kilnheadmen, For 537 lb Bells of Limeshulls @ 5/ p 100 £24 | 1 | 7
Received payment of the above. —
    Hen. Robertson

Drawers For drawing 11279 lb Shells & Sum @ 33 p 100 £ 18 | 6 | 4
Trimmers For trimming 7544 lb Shells Shipped @ 14d do 5 | „ | 7
Slackers, For manufacturing & Ship g 136 Cha.d @ 6½ p Cha.d 7 | 18 | 8
Emptiers, For empting 1647 Waggons of 3 tons @ 1/6 p 100 9 | 8 | 10
                     £ 40 | 14 | 5

Rec.d payment of the above £40.14.5
   John Addison   John Willet
   John Hugh   John Buchannan

J. Gen.l Oncost Limestone Shippers Rob.t Wells & Co
  for Shipping 2021 Tons of Limestone @ 1/4 p ton 11 | 12 | 5
  Sawyers for Sawing 2685 feet of hard
    Wood @ 4/6 p 100 —————— lb.. 7.
  & 1462 feet of fir @ 2/6 p 100 — 1.16.6½ 7 | 17 | 2
  Masons for amount of their wages — 14 | 14 | 4
  Wrights for amount of their wages — 21 | 1 | 4
  Petty expences for Bye Portages and
    sundry trifles ————————— 1 | 10 | .
                   £ 56 | 15 | 3

Received payment of the above
   George Dick
   James M'Lern   Thomas Lee
   Robert Wells

Overseers & Labourers for amount of their wages 88 | 6 | 4
Received payment of the above
           James Walker

WORKING CONDITIONS

This has been referred to as "The Hellish Scene". So what was it like to work here? Those working at the kilnhead lived in constant danger. They had to load the coal and limestone into the kiln with a barrow. The kiln was an open 12ft diameter hole at ground level. There was absolutely no protection and the area was covered in thick smoke and hot fumes. They had to work in a very small area round the kiln with little room to turn the barrow. This was at the edge of a 30 ft drop in front of the kilns with only a small rail as protection. A fall into the kiln or over the outer wall would almost certainly have proved fatal.

The drawers below fared little better. They had to operate in very hot, dusty conditions and, like the slakers, were also in danger of being burned by the quicklime. The day was long - often from 4 a.m. until 6 p.m. in the season. It is little wonder that the consumption of whisky was so high! One comfort was that there was a spring of cool clear water. No doubt this was in constant use - even by the horses since the trough was in one of the big openings. This water is reputed to have medical benefits and the local doctor, on a guided walk recently, remarked that it also was a cure for warts!

Harbour c1875

THE HARBOUR

Central to the whole success of the enterprise was Charlestown Harbour. Today this is only used by private boat owners and is full of mud when the tide is out. However the inquisitive observer can find many remnants of the time when this was a hive of activity with queues of ships waiting to be loaded with coal or lime. On either side of the harbour are ballast banks. Those were brought back from foreign parts by ships in ballast.

Coal Loading Straithes c1900

On those could be found plants and stones which are not indigenous to the area. The West bank is now covered with houses and the East, which dates from c1870, is a car park. Stumps of crane foundations can be seen. In the centre of the harbour there are the wooden bases of coal staithes, though there are two houses on top, which are completely out of place. On the far side one can see the decaying framework of a lighthouse at the harbour entrance. In a corner are the remains of the sluicing mechanism. What a story can be unearthed from this decay.

The building of the harbour was one of the first parts of the plan to be carried out. The inner harbour and pier were completed by 1761 using the sandstone from TODHOLE QUARRY which is adjacent. The first staithe had arisen in 1770. The inner harbour was much larger than what is there today. It came very close to the kilns: about midway across the road now in place. Of course the side of this harbour was vertical: the present sloping wall was built by the railway people over a century later to carry the line to their new station. This has somewhat obscured the very close relationship between the kilns and the harbour, which was a big factor in the success of the business. The proximity of the harbour to the kilns meant that lime shells, once they had cooled down, could be shovelled directly aboard a ship.

The COAL STAITHE is an interesting piece of machinery. Coal arrived on the wagonways by cart. At the staithe a wagon could be upended and the coal went down a shute into the ship. The staithes were reached by the railway in the 1820's and were still in use here in the early part of the 20th century.

From this harbour there was quite a bit of emigration. One could buy a ticket at the harbour office to any place in the world. Many folks left for the Empire - Australia, New Zealand and Canada. Some, like the Carnegies, opted for U.S.A.

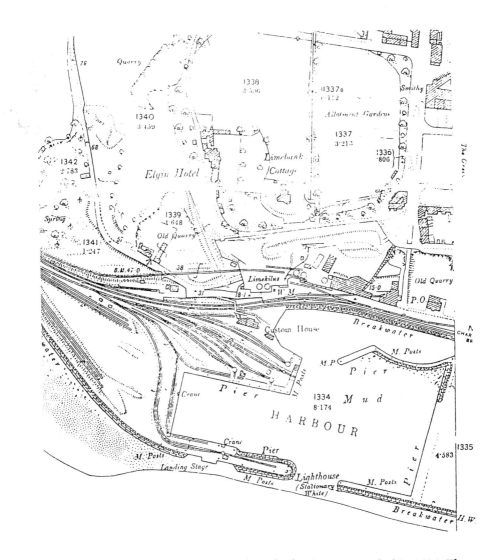

The trade was such that Lord Elgin had the harbour extended in 1824. There was also a sluicing mechanism introduced. This was rather ingenious so that, when the tide was in, a pond was filled and the gate shut. When the tide was out, this dam was opened and the rush of water flushed out the silt. There is now a tidal duck pond on the site.

The 1826 map shows the harbour at that point in time. There is the freestone quarry alongside and the railway over the viaduct has reached the coal staithes. East ballast bank has not then been started, but it was formed from 1850 onwards, and improvements went on until 1870.

By this time steam was beginning to be introduced, though for many years both steam and sail existed in lots of vessels. Passenger steamers called at Charlestown. At low tide the steamships could not use the harbour and passengers had to be rowed out. Many came down on the railway or walked there. In 1833 this had become a thriving service. The steamers ran between Granton (for Edinburgh) and Stirling calling at ports in between. Charlestown was one of the few ports on the North side of the river.

THE COAL TRADE

Lord Elgin leased and ran the pits of the Elgin collieries. Those lay around the West of Dunfermline at Wellwood, Clunie, Baldridge and Colton and by mid 19th century were producing 2000 tons per week. There were employed some 400 men and boys and 200 women and children. There were also pit ponies. The working conditions in mines in Scotland is another story. Much of this coal came down the coal railway to Charlestown.

There was little point in producing all of this fuel unless good use could be made of it. Locally it can be argued that many of the small industries round Charlestown grew up due to the need to find a use for the coal. e.g. the brickworks and foundry could use low grade, and the saltworks, sawmill and of course the kilns were customers.

However the bulk of the coal went for export from the harbour. There was a trade within Scotland to such places as the glassworks at Edinburgh, Leith, Alloa and Dumbarton. Some of this went via the Union canal system.

COKE

Coking kilns were at the East end of the complex against a high retaining wall. Coke is made by heating suitable coal in a closed coke oven or kiln. This is closed so that the oxygen cannot reach the coal otherwise it would burn. The volatile gas content of the coal is driven off. Hot coke has to be dowsed in water when it is drawn out so that it does not go on fire. At Charlestown salt water was used as it was at hand. 6 tons of coal yield 2 tons of coke. This coke was largely for export.

Large quantities of this fuel were shipped across Europe and even to Boston in U.S.A. It was found that Elgin coal was very suitable for steam engines and all of the steam-boats on the river Seine were powered by it. In excess of 10,000 tons annually was going to Europe, especially to Baltic ports of Germany, Russia, Denmark, Sweden and Norway. There is a bill of 1857 showing 168 tons shipped to Copenhagen. From those ports was imported timber from the Baltic and pantiles from Holland. Those were distributed by rail from Charlestown.

No. 287   **CHARLESTOWN,** 28ᵗʰ May 1857,
NEAR DUNFERMLINE.

Shipped from the Elgin Collieries,

on board the "Interessents Labet" of Thisted

N. Madsen   Master,

on Account and Risk of Joh: Theod. Salvesen Esq. Grangemouth; and bound for Copenhagen.

	Tons Elgin Household Coal,.............@	9/.	£
168	Tons Elgin Wallsend Coal, ...@		75 . 12/
	Tons Elgin Engine Coal, ...@		
	Tons Elgin Glasswork and Lime do.......@		

Cash advanced for Ship's use,...............@   £75 . 12/

Deduct
7 ⅌ Ct. Con discount _____ 4 . 17/

75 . 12/
70 . 15/

Charlestown 28ᵗʰ May 1857. By Bill
@ 1 m/d _____ £ 70 . 15/

28 — 5 — 1857.

This trade was very attractive to N.B.R. Co. when they took over ownership of the harbour in 1863. The coal trade receded from the harbour from then on. This was largely due to the expansion of the railway and the fact that Charlestown could not compete with such ports as Methil and Burntisland. By the turn of the century the coalfield round Dunfermline had decreased and by 1930 only Wellwood was left. The coal trade at Charlestown had reached ¼ million tons at its peak but by 1900 this had dropped to 35,000 tons. This became a trickle for local industries and coke manufature, and deep mining finished in mid 1960's.

Returning to the harbour itself. The railway company, immediately they secured the harbour, extended it by erecting the East pier and outer arm. This was completed by 1870 and this is the present form of the harbour.

The decline in trade led to the harbour being largely unused early in the 20th century. Fate was however to give it a new lease of life after the first World War. This was due to the arrival to the shipbreakers. This continued until 1963 with a break during the second World War. The harbour was requisitioned by the Admiralty. There were naval items stored and there were landing craft and midget sumarines berthed.

Currently this attractive but neglected place is a haven for private pleasure craft and the ballast bank is an excellent place to walk the dog. There are however ambitious plans afoot.

THE LIME TRADE ... SUCCESS?

We have looked at how this complex operated. Lime products came out of the works for 200 years, but there were advantages and disadvantages.

The biggest plus was the sheer volume produced. This meant that Charlestown could outsell any other competitor. This had to be the case to make the business viable. The site was first-class. The quarries were only ½ mile away and the harbour was adjacent. The Elgin railway, and earlier wagonways, brought the coal from the mines around Dunfermline, some 5 miles away. The kilns were constructed so that limestone and coal could be delivered directly to the kilnhead without any complicated lifting involved.

At this time the agricultural developments were largely in the Eastern parts of Scotland. Water travel was much better than carting loads on poor roads. So the transport of the lime by sea was a big factor and it was fairly easy to reach inland along the rivers to the heart of the farming areas. The completion of the Union and Forth and Clyde Canals in 1790 made this an important route to the west. In 1822 the Caledonian Canal allowed the highlands to be reached. On the minus side of sea travel was the fact that lime shells were a difficult cargo to carry in wooden ships. If it got wet, then the bottom of the boat could be burned out, and sometimes did, leading to disaster. Shipowners were encouraged to make deliveries as soon as possible!

Charlestown lime was much harder than its competitors. Sometimes it contained impurities and was not always fully burned. This led to some complaints from the farmers spreading the lime: they were told to employ workers to go around the fields and break it up. The demand however remained high. It did have good waterproofing properties and was used to build the docks at Dundee and Leith.

We have seen that the design of the kilns could certainly have been improved. So also could the way in which the workers were paid and organised.

The Earls, through the factors, were able to overcome those problems however. Firstly there was the enormous quantity of limeshell produced. Then there was the system of selling to the customers. They were given a bargain in both coal and lime in the shape of "The Charlestown Ton". Every 1 ton (20 cwts) ordered, became 21 cwts delivered. People were also given 6 months credit in which to settle. The lime was cheaper than elsewhere and the supplies were plentiful. There were selling agents appointed in towns like Dundee, Montrose, Aberdeen, Stirling and Alloa. This system of selling went on for the 120 years that the Estate ran the works directly. It ensured that Charlestown had an almost virtual monopoly in those places. The lime trading was by postal order. In the 18th century letters came and went ordering lime and coal and arranging transport. This was vital to the trading and was in force long before the arrival of the 1d universal postage stamp.

It has been argued that Scotland could not have the whisky industry it has today if it were not for Charlestown lime and the improvements made to the soil on which the barley is grown.

Charles Landale, an Engineer employed at the end of the 18th century and start of the 19th, kept making improvements to the quarrying, the workers bargains, the wagonway, the harbour and the kilns. This never really made the working anything other than 'hard graft. It did, though, ensure that the product was the cheapest to be had. It was this through-put which led to the continued success of Charlestown. For example, Charlestown could produce over 4,000 tons lime per worker in a year. This was about 3 times the rate of other works in Scotland.

In the later part of the 19th Century, the lime complex was leased out by the Estate. Eventually the CHARLESTOWN LIME CO was formed in 1890 and they were the operators until the works closed. There were 25 men employed in 1930. There are still one or two fellows about who worked in the kilns. They have told me that the bogies carrying the stone down the tunnel held 21 cwt: and that the extra cwt was the lairds rent!

LIME TO THE PITS

This trade was to continue right up to the end of the working life of the kilns. From 1935 limestone was being brought down from Roscobie. This lies about 10 miles to the North-East and was delivered by a lorry. Powdered lime from the crusher was sent to the pits around the area. There it was spread on the passages when blasting was to take place. The lime is heavier than the coal dust which it kept down and prevented explosions. This was a small but important and steady trade. For example, Valleyfield Colliery was using 2 tons per day in the 50's.

The final act took place in 1956 when the Lime Co sold off the vehicles and equipment. For a time one or two of the kilns were used for storage of coal. The buildings on the kilnhead were demolished but the kiln complex is still in place and looking good 250 years after being built and having had a hard life.

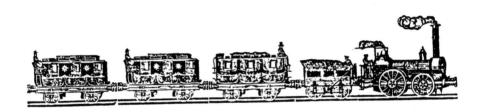

ELGIN RAILWAY

"... in the omnibus that ran on the coal road to Charlestown. I remember that I stood with tearful eyes....". So wrote the remarkable Andrew Carnegie as he recalled the first part of the journey to America in 1848 with his family as he left behind his beloved Dunfermline. So what was this omnibus? Where did it go? How was it powered? Who operated it? What remains of this coal road today? Well this was the Dunfermline to Charlestown railway which had developed from modest origins involving horses, to become a railway with steam engines, iron rails, passengers and bridges; as we think of a railway today.

NEW PASSAGE
TO GLASGOW.

FROM *Limekilns* to *Blackness*, at half-past Eight, morning, and Two, afternoon.

Blackness to *Limekilns*, at Ten, morning, and half-past Three, afternoon.

FARE, 6d *each person.* *Canal Boat*, 2s 6d.

By the morning passage, Travellers get to Glasgow at Four in the afternoon, by meeting the Canal Swift Boat at Fort Devon Bridge, about two miles above Blackness.

Passages across at other hours by engaging the Boat; and a low Water landing-place is now made on the south side.

Farther information given by Mr Mailler, Merchant, Limekilns.

Gala Day - waiting at Charlestown Station for the train to Dunfermline

The industrial developments taking place in the 18th century led to the need for this line. Coal had for many centuries been mined around Dunfermline and, as the need for it increased, clearly it had to be delivered to those industries. At this time the avenue was mainly by the sea. The nearest port was Brucehaven, on the outskirts of Limekilns. This was a distance of around 5 miles but the roads were inadequate and useless in bad weather. Some roads had been improved but the journey was slow, painful and expensive. The wagons were poorly constructed and pulled by horses or oxen. By the end of the 18th century heavy horses had largely replaced oxen as the favoured draught animal.

Alongside the coal requirements, in this area had arisen the lime industry and the developments at Charlestown. The demand for lime was increasing and coal was a vital ingredient in the making of quicklime. Those factors were to combine so that Earl Charles could see a clear case for the construction of a wagonway from the collieries to Limekilns (and later to Charlestown).

Lord Elgin did not at the time own all of the land on which to build. His neighbouring landowners were Sir John Wedderburn at Pitfirrane (later Sir John Halkett), Robert Wellwood of Garvock and Pitliver, and George Chalmers of Pittencrieff. There ensued years of wrangling and argument over the route. There was the direct route from the town to Brucehaven and also an alternative from Knockhouse and Urquhart through Crossford and Pitifirrane to Limekilns. Chalmers appears to have been the "difficult" landowner and the direct route was abandoned for the time being. Chalmers was later to become bankrupt. Construction started in 1774 on the longer route.

Earl Charles died in 1771 so he did not live to see this part of his grand plan completed. The Estate was for a time run by trustees since Earl Thomas was only 5 at this time. The Estate was effectively run by Martha, the Dowager Countess, Thomas' mother. The wagonway was at last completed. This had wooden rails and the motive power was the horse. The line ran from the pits at Berrielaw and Knockhouse through Crossford. Then the route led down via Meadowend and Craigs bank to Broomhall Estate. It passed east of Broomhall House and down to the village, behind the church and in front of Gardener's Cottage to reach Limekilns Harbour. There was a branch to Capernaum. In 1790 the line passed solely into the Earl's ownership. For a time the coal had to be carted the ½ mile to the kilns from Limekilns village. A spur was built from Broomhall later to end behind the Old Inn at the top of the "Run". To get down to the harbour was a steep incline. The method used had full wagons going down pulling empties coming up on an endless rope. This ingenious method would have been spectacular.

The RUN or ROPAREE is now a walkaway down to the harbour. provided an exciting place to go sledging in winter - lads have been known to finish up rather wet in the harbour!

The possibility of constructing a new line on the original direct route again came up. There were still legal difficulties, now with Mr Hunt as owner of Pittencrieff. Another was that Earl Thomas was engaged in foreign affairs abroad and had been detained in France from 1802-06. On his return he was able to turn his attention to his railway. Eventually most legal matters were settled by 1809, through negotiations were still going on until 1820.

In the meantime the wooden rails on the old line were replaced with iron ones.

This made life much easier for the horses: 100 of them became redundant because of this improvement. The new railway had iron rails from the start.

The work started at the Charlestown end in 1795 and an attractive 3 arch VIADUCT was built in 1810 so that the harbour could be reached directly for the first time. This bridge may well be the first in Scotland built specifically to carry a railway. There are other rivals but in most cases the bridge was already in place for the wagonway to upgrade to a railway. The viaduct is a listed monument and is due for a facelift in the near future. This new cutting ran down the Shell Road (quicklime is often referred to as shell) to the harbour with a branch to the kilnhead.

The new line reached Dunfermline at the foot of the Coal Road in 1812. The old line through Crossford was closed. There were still problems to be resolved so that the line could reach the collieries but the 1823 O.S. map shows this achieved. The line now ran from the Elgin pits all the way to the harbour. At the Dunfermline end there was an incline from Colton (end of Grieve Street) down to where the Crossford road crosses William Street. Another ran from this intersection on Pittencrieff Street down to the bottom of the Coal Road. Loaded wagons would thunder down those whilst pulling up the unladen ones. Present day folks wonder why there is that dangerous right angled bend at the foot of the Coal Road. Well of course at the time of the railway it carried straight on. There was an interchange here and the wagons were coupled to horses.

A wagon carried over 4 tons of coal and could easily be pulled on the iron rails by horses on the level but assistance was required on the steeper parts. There were two rope-worked inclines on the route with stationary steam engines. One was situated in Meadowend and the other down the incline at Fiddlershall.

Up until now the railway had been only concerned with freight, largely coal. In 1834 Earl Thomas is reputed to have himself designed a passenger omnibus. This was still horse drawn and carried 50 people. Probably it was not a very comfortable ride but here we have the beginning of the passenger service by rail in Scotland. A branch line was made to the terminus at the top of Elgin Street between Forth Street and the drill hall. At the Charlestown end the station was alongside the old Elgin Hotel (now Camsle House). At present there is a tennis court on the station foundation and the Broomhall Cricket Club pitch covers the line. This innovation meant that folks from the town could have a day at the seaside for 6d (2p) with children at half price. It was on this railway that the Carnegie family left for America. In 1852 steam engines were introduced to the line. Those were only allowed for freight at first as it was regarded as too dangerous for passengers. However we did not have the man with the proverbial red flag. The Board of Trade tested the 3 drivers for their skill:- 1) a clean pass, 2) average, 3) on no account whatever! ... passengers soon followed.

The 1856 map shows the line at its zenith-from the collieries down William Street, across Pittencrieff Street, down the side of the Glen with a branch to Netherton Station. Then the route was to Liggars Bridge where there was an engine shed. Then the present line is followed to Merryhill. The line ran on the South side of Lochymuir whereas the old line had been on the North side. The line ran alongside the present road to Fiddlershall with a branch leading off to the Charlestown Brick and Tile Co. There was a three way junction at Fiddlershall corner. The old line ran from here under a bridge at the Ginhead and round the laundry corner to the top of the run. The harbour line ran down the Shell Road and over the viaduct. The passenger line ran across the present cricket pitch to the station at Camsie.

This then was the line which became known as the Elgin Railway. It had been the property of the Broomhall Estate for a century, but the time came in 1863 for the Estate to shed some of its ventures. The North British Railway Co purchased the harbour and railway. Passenger traffic was discontinued but the coal trade rose to 230,000 tons per year. The harbour was extended to the East. The incline over the viaduct was proving too steep for steam locos and the bend at the foot was too sharp. The line was realigned at Merryhill along a new cutting and causeway to the harbour. A passenger station was built at the Saltpans (where no.1 is today) and services re-established in 1894. They were to last until 1938. At the town end Comely Bank Station was built and a new line built to Netherton. Some bits of the old railway route were left and recently it has come to light that the ½ mile stretch, Elbow junction past Meadowend to Lochymuir, is the oldest route in Scotland still in use.

Meanwhile N.B.R. had decided to build a rail bridge across the 2 ½ miles of the Forth from Charlestown to Blackness. Sir Thomas Bouch made elaborate plans and the agreement of Parliament was obtained. The plan never really got off the ground and Bouch called it off after problems with the mud off Braeside. The bridge would have been of similar construction to the Tay Bridge and would probably have met the same fate. The Company decided to be safe and erected the massive over-engineered bridge at Queensferry.

Work began at the Crombie Armament Depot in 1911 and a branch was built into it, which resulted in the canal being filled in. This was served by a halt at Shillinghill. N.B.R. amalgamated in 1923 to be incorporated in L.N.E.R. and then B.R. in 1948 upon Nationalisation. Trade decreased at the harbour and when shipbreaking ceased, B.R. had no further use for the harbour which was bought back into the Estate in mid 60's.

In its day the Elgin railway was of major significance in the industrial and social development of the area and particularly Charlestown village. Unfortunately this has largely been forgotten locally. Folks walk their dogs along the shell road cutting and over the viaduct with no idea that this was once a railway.

The depot at Crombie has ensured that the line is still open... occasionally we even get a train along it. Usually this is only a loco and 2 wagons! Twice in our history the Charlestown to Dunfermline Railway has carried passengers, only to lose the facility. Perhaps in the future this 4 miles of track will again conduct good folks to the model village.

CHAPTER THREE

THE MODEL VILLAGE

CHARLESTOWN VILLAGE

Maps of the area of the early 1700's show Broomhall and Lymekilns, but no sign of Charlestown. There were dwellings at Turnershill and Maryhill. Charles' eye settled on the area known as Whalebank for his model village. A glance at the attached map will show how the plan was implemented. Since everything was starting from scratch, it will be clear that the works, quarries, wagonways, harbour and houses had to be set in motion simultaneously. They were all interdependent and as workers and families were recruited, they had to have accommodation.

Once cleared, the site for this model village resembled a level plateau 60 feet above the harbour. The foundations are solidly planted on sandstone (see Tod-Hole Quarry). The building started in 1756 and went at a cracking pace. By 1771, South Row, Lochaber and part of North Row were built. Major General John Scott's map of 1775 shows Charlestown emerging for the first time - the village was born.

Double Row c1900 - note the bare feet

The architectural plan was quite simple. The houses were arranged in rows set to form the initials of the founder CE. (Actually the Bruce family has always considered this to be KE - Kincardine then Elgin). The Queens Hall is central on the C and Lochaber and Hall Row form the two arches. North Row and South Row are the two outer arms of the E and the Double Row the shorter centre one. The Cross Row connects the three arms. All of the Rows have houses on only one side except the Double Row. In the space between the North and South Rows is the Foals Park. This is usually referred to as the 'Village Green' and generations of children have played there. Today it contains children's playing equipment. The houses were originally all of the same size and were built in sets of 6 i.e. 6 houses then a close, then another 6... The closes all have names, the most used one is Peggy Bell's Brae, after the lady who lived at the top of it.

The cottages are small by modern standards: living-room, bedroom and kitchen. The ceilings were, and still are, low and the floors were earthen. Later square brick floors were laid and this lasted up to 1920. The roofs were uniformly red pantiles. The original ones were imported from the Continent but later they were produced at Charlestown Brick and Tile Co. There was no running water or sanitation. This could be regarded as squalor but Elgin housing was of a higher standard than most and was a big improvement on previous dwellings in the land.

Water had to be carried from wells initially, then the Estate in 1840 had water piped to 6 wells at strategic points in the village. Those may still have been at some distance from an individual house and it was not until well into the 1920's that water was piped to each house.

Each home had an outside privvy, often at the foot of the garden. There is a story that a visitor complained to his host that "there is no lock on the door". This was met with the reply "I have never lost a pailful yet".

THE HONEY CART

The collection of raw sewage, known as Police Work in old Scots parlance, was one of the problems facing Lord Elgin. This was solved and the "little houses" at the foot of the garden were emptied into a cart and the resultant compost spread on the field behind Fiddlershall. To this day, this field grows the best crops in the area!

This practice continued well into this century when the operator was one Wull Cant. His horse drawn vehicle was affectionately known, for obvious reasons, by the villagers as the "honey cart".

There are many tales of Wull... this is one:- One very warm summer's day he was going about his business and had hung his jacket on the cart which had high sides. Sometime later he was spotted by two village worthies hanging over the side of the cart with only his legs showing. "What are you up to in there", he was asked. The reply was "My jaiket has fallen inside". That's disgusting; forget it and come oot o' there." "But my piece is in my pocket!"

Laws and Regulations

FOR THE PROPER GOVERNMENT OF

THE VILLAGE OF

CHARLESTOWN,

Which has been built & is kept up exclusively for the purpose of accommodation to the Works belonging to the Right Honourable **Thomas** *Earl of* **Elgin** *and* **Kincardin.** *viz.*

I.

THE said Earl shall have power to remove any person or family from his or her dwelling-house and yard, in the said village, at the Martinmas term, on one Calendar month's previous notice; AND to remove any person or family, from his or her house and yard, foresaid, at the Whitsunday term, on two Calendar month's previous notice, to be given in writing, to be delivered either into the hands of the person or family to be removed, or left in his or her house; which shall be a sufficient and final warning, without the necessity of assigning any reason for so doing, or without regard to the term of entry.

II.

ON THE OTHER HAND, it shall be in the power of any person or family, possessing a house and yard in said village, to remove at Martinmas, or Whitsunday, as he or she may chuse, on a similar previous notice, of one and two Calendar months; to be delivered at the office in writing, signed by the person or persons, intending to remove, and addressed to the said Earl: which shall be esteemed a sufficient intimation. AND, such houses and yards as are thus given up, will be let to others accordingly.

III.

IF a person, or family, shall possess a house and yard in said village, for a year, or years, from Martinmas to Martinmas; such person, or family, must pay a full year's rent of house and yard, on or before Martinmas day, for the first year, and so forth yearly during such period, and mode of possession. BUT, any person, or family, removed, or coming from a house and yard in said village at the Whitsunday term, shall, on or before the Whitsunday term day, pay only a half year's rent of the house: AND his, or her successor shall, on or before the next Martinmas day, pay a half year's rent of the house, and a whole year's rent of the yard; and so forth yearly and termly in like manner.

IV.

EVERY inhabitant of said village, while not in actual employment at the works, must make punctual payment of his or her house and yard rent, in terms foresaid, on the Whitsunday and Martinmas term days, at or before noon of such day; by half-yearly payments; otherwise it shall be in the power of the said Earl to remove any person failing herein from his or her house and yard, the day following such omission; and to let the same to others. AND it shall be in the power of his Lordship to stop and retain the house and yard rents, of all the inhabitants in said village, immediately employed in the works, out of their pay, passing through his hands, by half yearly or yearly payments, to be taken by him as he sees they have it best to spare. AND he is not to be confined to their time, but may retain a half year's rent at or before Whitsunday, and the balance of house and yard rent at any time between Whitsunday and the end of September, so as to have the whole year's rent paid by that period.

V.

Whereas every person engaged at the works subscribes a certain portion of each pay towards the maintenance of a School, at which all the Children of the village and works receive Education without the usual charge for fees;— Every inhabitant of the village though not immediately employed at the works, or receiving pay from the office, is nevertheless bound to contribute to this fund, and to be entitled to the advantage of it; and therefore is bound to pay towards it, on the first day of every month, in the following proportion on their rent :
viz.—If from 18s to 24s, to pay One Shilling per month;
If from 24s to 30s, to pay Two Shillings per month;
If from 30s and upwards, to pay Three Shillings per month.

VI.

NO retail trade whatever, is to be carried on, without a specific agreement to that effect, in any house in CHARLESTOWN. IF any attempt be made to contravene this prohibition, the said Earl shall have power to put a stop to it instantly, and to remove the inhabitant from the house and from the village, within eight days after the breach of this Law. AND such persons as transgress herein, must pay rent for both house and yard up to the ensuing term, if the offence is committed at the lapse of one Calendar month after the term.

VII.

THE said Earl will uphold the walls, roofs, doors, window-cases, and all fixed work of the houses, in said village, while they are not destroyed wilfully, or through neglect. THE inhabitants must keep in repair the glass of their windows, and the keys of their doors; and they must leave the windows whole, and deliver up a key fit to open and lock their doors, at their removal.

VIII.

EVERY person possessing a house in said village, must regularly every morning, clear the water channels, and rake and sweep the whole street immediately opposite to his or her house; must pare up all grass, and gather together the whole dung and fulzie produced by him or her into the place appropriated for each house respectively.

IX.

EVERY inhabitant of the village, is hereby allowed to use any part he or she chuses of his or her dung or fulzie, in the first place, for the use of their respective yards. BUT the whole inhabitants, without exception, are strictly prohibited from giving away or selling any part of his or her dung or fulzie to any person, except to the said Earl, without leave asked and obtained in writing, for every occasion severally. AND it is expressly declared, that the inhabitants aforesaid, are hereby bound and obliged to sell the whole of their dung and fulzie, after serving their yards, (what they may forfeit in manner preceding also excepted) to the said Earl at the current rate of the country. AND every inhabitant acting contrary to this Law, so disposed of contrary to this law, for each cart load, or portion thereof, so disposed of contrary to this law, to the said Earl, who is hereby authorized to levy such sums immediately on conviction.

X.

THE inhabitants must be careful that the fences along the streets and gardens, and the shrubberies, are not broken down, or injured by them, their children, their pigs, or poultry. BECAUSE, any such damage will be instantly repaired at the expense of the inhabitants, opposite whose house any damage is done; unless such inhabitants shall convict others of the offence.

XI.

THE inhabitants are, moreover, specially warned, for themselves and their children :—

a Not to do any damage to the trees, hedges, pailings, fences, or shrubberies, in or about the village.

b Not to enter or pass through any of the plantations or enclosures.

c Not to do any injury to the gardens or crops on the neighbouring lands.

d Not to allow any pigs, or poultry to stray beyond the premises of the inhabitants to whom they belong.

e Not to carry off, or remove out of its place, or meddle with, any wood, coal, iron, barrows, waggons, working implements, machinery, or any thing whatever, on Lord Elgin's property.

f Not to pilfer coals from the waggons, the deposits, or sea shore, or allow their children to do so.

g And not to neglect to keep their children out of mischievous practices and idleness, particularly on the Sabbath day.

For any of the above, or similar transgressions, the inhabitants shall be prosecuted as the Law directs. AND moreover, they shall be fined in a penalty, not exceeding Two Shillings and Sixpence for each offence, committed by them or their children : That penalty to be immediately appropriated to the uses of such fund, intended for the good of the inhabitants of the village, as Lord Elgin shall point out.

XII.

IT is the special duty of the constables, and the overseers at the works, to enforce a constant observance of the above Regulations, and to report on every offence, as soon as it is discovered.

XIII.

AS a printed copy, in all respects similar to this, of the above Laws and Regulations, has been pasted up in every house in said village, none of the inhabitants can, as heretofore, pretend ignorance. AND they are required to preserve said laws from abuse or destruction. AND, if it shall happen that, through any unseen accident, they are destroyed, upon application at the Office another copy will be given gratis: BUT, if it appears, upon reasonable grounds, that they are abused or destroyed through inattention or design, IN THAT CASE, the person, under whose roof this happens, must not only apply for another copy, that they may be preserved in every house, till the said Earl sees proper to alter them, but the person applying on this account must pay Two Shillings sterling for the copy he or she may receive.

By appointment of the said EARL.

OFFICE at CHARLESTOWN,
OCTOBER, 1815.

Printed by J. Miller, Dunfermline

The little houses were used until mains sewage reached the village. In 1930 the Estate equipped each house with water toilets. Some tenants fitted baths which were considered an unnecessary luxury. There is still one outside loo in use today - the owners find it convenient when gardening!

Gas did not arrive until 1908 although Dunfermline had been lit by gas from 1829: so it took 80 years to come 4 miles. Apparently the villagers were offered gas lighting about 1870 but the offer was turned down because "when it was dark people should go to bed".

All of the houses had a garden or yard. This was either at the front of the house or at the rear or sometimes both. Tenants were all allowed to keep an animal - usually a pig or two and a few hens - in the yard. This all helped to feed the family. There are still a few hens about the place, but generally the practice has ceased and for many years the yards have been productive gardens. Indeed for much of this century Charlestown has been renowned for its garden produce.

The village has a rather quaint and unusual method of house numbering. Each has an original number e.g. no 87 Charlestown. This does not reflect the street at all, so that every house has 2 numbers - one according to the Row and another of the village. One may find no 67 next door to no 5. Many of the folks refuse to change from the original number. This is all very confusing to the visitor but all attempts to change this over the years have been unsuccessful.

In 1815, Earl Thomas produced his "LAWS AND REGULATIONS" for Charlestown. Those set conditions for tenancy of the house and make compelling reading. Amongst other things it:-

Made deductions for attendance of children at school prohibited trade from a house without agreement of Estate encouraged people to keep the area tidy and in good repair forbade people to sell or give away any dung except to the Earl encouraged folk not to steal but to keep their children in order There were heavy fines for breaking the rules, which were enforced by the constables and overseers.

Continuing round the village and built about the same time, we arrive at the Granary building which incorporates the Sutlery. Next to this is the village School and on the opposite side of the road were stables. On the corner stood the Laundry and Bleaching Green. This was a great place for the ladies of the place to have a gossip; it certainly continued to be so when the Fotheringhams ran it! The Estate Workshops and Blacksmith's Shop stood on the other corner. All of those buildings will be discussed later.

At the end of West Road is FIDDLERSHALL. This is reputed to be the oldest residence in the village. It was once 4 dwelling houses, but it was recently converted into a large single one. Opposite is the site of FLOWRIEHALL or the BLUEHOOSE, now occupied by a modern bungalow. There have been 3 hotels or inns in the village. The OLD INN is now the Estate Office. In posting days, horses used to be changed at Charlestown Inn. The building has had three different uses since then and even housed the district nurse. CAMSIE HOUSE was in part the ELGIN ARMS INN from 1790 until 1911. It was also a bakery for quite a time. The new ELGIN HOTEL was erected in 1911 at a cost of £3600. It was owned by the Estate with tenants running it until fairly recently when it was sold and has had extensive renovation and improvements since then.

EASTER COTTAGE is a very attractive building. It was so called because of its situation just to the East of the harbour. Recently discovered evidence in the Broomhall archives indicates that the house was built circa 1813-1814 for the Limekilns manager, Charles Landale and his successors, the last of these being William Black. The house was originally thatched. The 1858 map lists the places of interest as the Elgin Arms Inn, Easter Cottage and the Sawmill opposite. There was actually a corresponding Wester Cottage, also thatched. It is said that it burned down after hot coal landed on it from a passing train. It is now a ruin in the grounds of Braeside.

The houses at the CAIRNS were built just after the 2nd World War on what was the football pitch for the illustrious Broomhall Football Club. The players had their Stripping Box behind the laundry and were a successful Junior Club. They played for some years on the village green after the Cairns were built but gradually petered out of existance. Just to prove the point that something else will spring up to replace what is lost; in the field next to the Cairns, Broomhall Cricket Club has been resurrected after many years and we now have a cricket square and pavilion.

The new housing at SALTPANS was erected from 1970 as were those on West Harbour. The development at ROCKS ROAD on the laundry site was developed from 1980.

Between 1900 and 1907 considerable sums were spent by the Estate on renovating the houses in Charlestown. By 1935 most of the houses in the village were rented from the Estate by families no longer in the employment of the Earl. It was decided to sell all of the houses at very competitive prices to sitting tenants. The prices varied between £15 and £35. Most of the offers were taken up and only a handful of the properties are still owned by the Estate. The houses of today have all been modernised and most have sprouted extensions. The purchase price when one comes on the market is often over £50,000... more than 1000 times the original offer! Charlestown is now a Conservation Area.

CHARLESTOWN SCHOOL

By the start of the 18th century, schools were beginning to spring up in Scotland. The Scottish Parliament had encouraged this, but there was no national organisation or funding. Education was not really taken seriously or regarded as important: so the standard was very low or non-existent. This sad state of affairs did not accord with the lofty ideas of culture and learning of the creator of Charlestown. Early in the building of the village, a purpose built school was erected in 1768 and this was going strong by 1770.

The building is two storey standing next to the Granary. It served the village for two centuries and still looks good today, although it was closed to pupils in 1968 when Charlestown ran out of sufficient pupils to make it viable. Primary pupils are now accommodated at Limekilns.

Class of 1910

The school was run by the Estate i.e. they erected the building, appointed and paid the schoolmaster, bought the equipment and encouraged the children to attend. In the beginning the attendance was poor as it was not compulsary, but this changed when the Earl deducted 1d per week from the men's wages. Inspectors' reports recorded that attendance was very high, though there were still a few non-attenders who were "loose up the woods".

There were really only two classrooms in the building, though the upper floor was used for handicrafts. The largest number of pupils recorded as attending was 238. Classes were large, often as much as 70. This can be set against the modern Secondary School where the pupil/teacher ratio is around 15. The school at this time, and almost to the end of the 19th century, was a complete entity-there was no Primary/Secondary divide, only one school. Peter Chalmers in his book records 32 schools, with 37 teachers and 2622 students in Dunfermline Parish in 1884. This gives a ratio of 71:1.

This will seem to be impossible to the teachers of today. How was it accomplished? There were probably two main reasons. Firstly some of the older children were designated PUPIL/TEACHERS. There are no records of how many such assistants there were, but clearly they were essential. The other factor was surely discipline. There was established strong order, generally by liberal use of the tawse or lochgelly. I can recall that at Primary School it was regarded as unusual if you didn't "get the belt" at least once every day!

In 1826 James Blyth was the schoolmaster and he was paid £36 for the ½ year. He gave £5 of this to his daughter as his assistant. James was succeeded in 1830 by his son George who was to teach in Charlestown for 45 years until he retired in 1875 with a 'liberal pension from the School Board in appreciation of his work.'

Prior to the arrival of the Queens Hall in 1887, the school was the centre of activities in the village. They had their own band and held concerts and dances. The schoolmaster also kept a library for use of the parents.

The curriculum was the basic 3 R's of Arithmetic, Reading and Writing. In addition the boys were taught trigonometry, for use in seamanship and mining surveying. The girls had instruction in sewing and embroidery.

The Estate continued to run the school until 1863. The Education Act of 1861 improved the lot of teachers and the school-house was built for the master. A Parochial board was formed and another Act of 1872 rationalised all of this and a compulsory system of Education was established. Nationally many buildings had to be built, but the school at Charlestown lived on under new control. We can claim that the introduction of this organised education for all had been achieved in Charlestown 100 years earlier.

BROOMHALL
MUTUAL IMPROVEMENT
SOCIETY.

AN ENTERTAINMENT
OF VOCAL & INSTRUMENTAL MUSIC
WILL BE GIVEN
IN LIMEKILNS SCHOOLROOM,
ON THE EVENING OF
FRIDAY, the 9th February 1877.

Programme---Part First.

OVERTURE,	...	...		...	COMPANY.
OPENING CHORUS,	...	...	"Happy are we Darkies, so gay,"	...	Mr J. DAWSON.
SONG,	...	...	"Mother would comfort me,"	...	Mr J. THOMSON.
COMIC SONG,	...	...	"Such a getting upstairs,"	...	Mr W. BARBER.
COMIC SONG,	...	...	"Pull back,"	...	Mr A. M'GREGOR.
SONG,	...	...	"Good old Jeff,"	...	Mr D. WILSON.
COMIC SONG,	...	...	"I'm off to Charleston,"	...	Mr W. PITBLADO.

SELECTION OF AIRS.

COMIC SONG,	...	...	"Old Bob Ridley,"	...	Mr A. M'GREGOR.
SONG,	...	...	"Poor old Joe,"	...	Mr D. WILSON.
COMIC SONG,	...	...	"Ring, ring de Banjo,"	...	Mr W. BARBER.
COMIC SONG,	...	...	"Funny little Nigger,"	...	Mr W. PITBLADO.
SONG,	...	...	"Sunny Ohio,"	...	Mr J. THOMSON.
COMIC SONG,	...	...	"Mulligan Guards,"	...	Mr J. DAWSON.

PART SECOND.
DIALOGUE.

COMIC SONG,	...	...	"I'll live as long as I can,"	...	Mr J. DAWSON.
BANJO SONG,	...	...	"Ober dere,"	...	Mr D. WILSON.
COMIC SONG,	...	...	"Josephus Orange Blossom,"	...	Mr J. DAWSON.

SELECTION OF AIRS.

FINALE,	...	...	"Plantation Walk,"	...	COMPANY.

Doors Open at 7.15 ; Chair to be taken at 7.45.
ADMISSION---Front Seats, 6d. ; Back, 3d.

PRINTED BY A. ROMANES, AT THE "PRESS" STEAM PRINTING WORKS, DUNFERMLINE.

The Headmaster from 1876 was James Davidson. When he first came to the village he lodged in the 'Blue Hoose' (Flowriehall) until the new Schoolhouse was ready for him. He had started as a pupil teacher for 5 years in Perth. During his time there he had taught Reading, Arithmetic, Grammar, Analysis, Geography, British History, Composition, Latin & Drawing. All of this was from an uncertificated lad! This experience was to lead him to succesfully completing a 2 year course of training at the Free Church Training College at Moray House. There he became qualified to "impart instruction" in Latin, Greek, English, Geography, History, Political Economy, Physical Science, Drawing, Magnetism and Electricity, Navigation, Physical Geography, Agriculture, Acoustics, Light, Heat, Religious Instruction, Singing, Mathematics and Experimental Physics. He was thus allowed to hold the Office of Teacher in an Elementry School under Goverment Supervision. No wonder that the bairns in Charlestown were so well educated.

Inspections of Charlestown school gave reports:-

1878 "The school is faithfully conducted and makes a very good appearance".

1879 "The school continues to be faithfully taught, with good general efficiency".

1880 "The school is conducted with excellent order and highly creditable general efficiency".

1925 "It is gratifying to record that the work accomplished here is so good as it actually is".

1937 "Periodically a costume play is produced for the benefit of the school fund, the children engaging in their parts wholeheartedly".

"The classroom is heated by a small open fire and this is quite inadequate, as is shown on the date of inspection the thermometer stood at 34F (just above freezing point)." Little wonder the children acted with gusto!

Other notable headteachers were Miss Louise Anderson (big Louis) 1919-, Miss Richie 1933-, Miss Euphemia Marshall 1953-65, and the last was Mrs Jean ('fingers') Carter 1965-68.

We still have the last school log book. To qualify for an entry in this tome, a pupil had to be very naughty, very sick or pass the entry exam to the High School. Many of my ancestors gained mentions and not for the latter reason. There were many notifiable illnesses about: diphtheria (2 brothers died from this in 1915), scarlet fever, whooping cough, measles, tuberculosis, mumps (there was an epedemic in 1921), St Vitas dance and chicken-pox.

The school was visited by the School Board (Managers) who were prominent local folks e.g. Mr Moodie (Compulsory Officer), Hugh Livingstone (Estate Factor), Mr Morton (Foundry Proprietor).

Behind the school was the grassy playground. Here generations of weans played such games as football, rounders, leavie-oh, tig, marbles, bebs, skipping etc. There also was a set of outside, very draughty, loos.

All public holidays are listed: Empire Day, Victoria Day, Gala Day in the Glen. There were events leading to a day off:- Royal wedding 1923, Visit of H.R.H. Prince of Wales 1933, V.E. Day 1945 etc.

The roll of the school was up to 144 during World War I when pupils from Crombie and Torryburn attended. However it fell steadily after that. In 1954 the roll was 28 and the school became 1 teacher. The decline continued and in 1968 the children and their teacher were moved to Limekilns Primary. Certainly those who were pupils in the early days were priviliged in comparison with the rest of the country. Former pupils remember the place with affection, despite the tawse. The building still stands proudly above Rocks Road awaiting someone to come along and find a new use for it.

Hygienic Laundry, Charlestown, Fife.

*Telephone
Limekilns
27.*

*How the lady can spend the
hours the Laundry gives her.*

**Send it to the
Laundry!**

CHARLESTOWN LAUNDRY

The cleaning of clothes was a big problem in those times. The dirty clothes were firstly boiled in a tub. This was brick built with a coal fire underneath. This meant an early start on washing day as the fire had first to be set and lit. This was primitive but the tub could double as a bath! Soap and bleach were added and the boiling mass stirred with a long wooden ladle. The energetic lady would also scrub the dirties on a board. This process took about 2 hours per load. Clothes were then rinsed in cold water and "mangled". The mangle was a contraption where the clothes were passed through two rollers turned by hand using a cast iron wheel with a handle: big muscles were required. There was then the problem of drying. If the weather was fine this could be done outside, otherwise hanging round the fire or in the kitchen. After all of this the clothes had still to be ironed using a hand-iron heated on a stove or in front of the fire. Therefore the good-lady had to spend a large part of her week in keeping her family cleanly dressed.

Today, with the push of a button, a machine can accomplish all of this, leaving much leisure time!

In Charlestown this was compounded by the nature of the work, as men were mostly employed in the quarries, kilns, harbour and railway: dirty work. It was difficult to hang out the washing to dry as the village was more or less permanently covered by a pall of smoke and effluent from the kilns. The prevailing wind from the West meant that this was a big problem. Lord Elgin c1770 was able to ease this burden by building a laundry and drying green to the North of the works and well away from the yellow cloud. For around a century this operated rather like the Glasgow steamy and the women were able to use the facilities to wash their clothes and then bleach/dry them on the green opposite.

The laundry was part of a complex of buildings built opposite the Granary on the corner of West Road and Rocks Road (Stable Row). Joined to the laundry was the village DAIRY and on the other side the DRILL HALL. Behind was the CORN-YARD, where Davie Elder kept his cuddy and also the STRIPPING BOX, the home of Broomhall football club.

The equipment in the laundry by the end of the 19th century included a steam boiler, a set of washing tubs, the standard Victorian drying, chamber and a stove to heat the hand-irons.

HYGIENIC LAUNDRY

In 1902 my grandfather, William Fotheringham, was persuaded by the Laird to take on this venture and run it on a commercial basis. William was a native of Cairneyhill as was his wife Isabella McDonald and both families were engaged in market-gardening.

Laundry with 'tunnel' in background 1912

The couple were married in 1895 and at the time Grannie F was working as a laundress in Govan. Probably this experience was to germinate the idea and later set the high standards for which the Hygienic Laundry became known.

There is the belief that Victorian families were large. This is probably a misconception as, with low wages, most men married later in life and could not afford many children. However this family was certainly large with 9 children - in chronological order - William, Annie, Ella, John, Norman, Harry, Winnie, Pearl and Dowsie. It is interesting to speculate on how the small houses in Charlestown coped. The house at the laundry had 2 bedrooms, a living room and a tiny kitchenette. One can only imagine how 11 people coped... 6 people per bedroom. There was a very small toilet, but there was the very first bath to be installed in Charlestown. This was a cast iron job located in the kitchen. It had a removable worktop on which food had to be prepared.

It is also worth recording the improvements in Medical provision over the last century by taking this family as an example:-

Grandfather William developed a septic tooth in 1922 and the poison went through his body leaving him with a useless left arm.

His wife died in 1923 (aged 49) from a haemorrhage. Annie died in 1939 (aged 41) from a heart attack after swimming.

Harry had a congenital heart defect and died in 1913 (aged 6).

Winnie died aged 12 in 1924 from a burst appendix before she reached hospital.

Pearl and Dowsie were both diabetics and died from associated problems aged 27 and 50 respectively.

It is probable that all of those lives would have been fulfilled given modern care.

ASHING GREEN, HYGEINIC LAUNDRY, CHARLESTOWN. N°4,10

In the early days laundry was collected by a pony named Bess and trap. They went as far as Dollar. Then there were Crossley motor vehicles. John and Norman were car enthusiasts and in the late 20's had a Sunbeam. This was a monster of a car with a dickie seat and could accommodate 8 in comfort. This vehicle could be hired to village lads to do their courting and cost 5/- (25p) for the afternoon and 10/- per day, the rate included petrol.

Much of the laundry trade was with the Navy at Rosyth. As a small lad I was able during the war to get on board many famous warships with my uncle to collect and deliver the dobbien. I can recall such as H.M.S. Rodney, Nelson, Illustrious etc. and later in life I was to join the Royal Navy. The

Crossley van used then was a wonderful vehicle. It had a hidden smuggling compartment under the dashboard where cigarettes and bottles of alcohol could be secreted.Those were later shared out with the sailors outside the main gate. Later we had a fleet of 3 vans beautifully hand-painted in maroon and gold: the Elgin colours.

Equipment made progress:- the tub became the washing-machine, the mangle the extractor, the fresh air the tumble dryer and the hand-iron the calender. What had been hours and hours of sweat could be removed by simply leaving a bundle for the laundryman to collect.

In the late 50's a drycleaning plant was added and by this time the laundry had expanded to cover all of this corner site and an extension built into the yard.

This was essentially a family business with all of the members employed in it. The oldest son William later moved to his grandfather's house Egypt in Cairneyhill from which he ran a fruit business. Otherwise all of the family spent their working lives engaged in laundering. Up to 20 local folks were employed, mainly female referred to as "the laundry lassies". Two in particular spent all of their time, from the age of 13 until retirement Effie Wilson and Bab Ferguson.

Progress again caught up and by 1970 the housewife had a home laundry. The business closed and the buildings reverted to the Estate. So the last employer in Charlestown closed down and two centuries of laundering on this site came to an end.

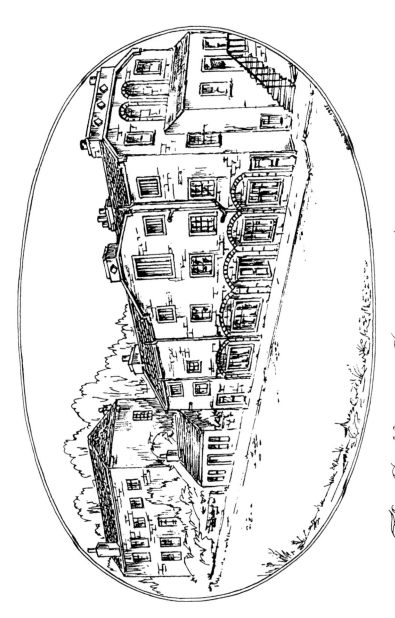

~ The Sutlery & Granary, Charlestown. 1805 ~
Former Company Victualling Store for Industries & Agriculture ~

GRANARY BUILDING

This is the largest building in the village and dates from 1770. It is properly called the Granary but it is usually referred to as the Sutlery, which is the general merchants and post-office on the ground floor. The first floor is residential flats and the top floor is the Granary.

The earliest usage of the ground floor can be seen from the appearance of the front of the building. The arches have now been filled in but the usage as stables is evident. At the time when the building was erected, oxen were often used as draught animals. Earl Thomas, from his travels abroad, brought back some bulls thinking to improve the transport system. However the animals proved to be very lazy and the experiment was a failure.

The HEAVY HORSE had largely replaced oxen by the end of the 18th century. Little has been said about these wonderful animals which were so long a vital part of the operation. Literally hundreds of horses (mainly Clydesdales) were used to pull wagons on the wagonways from the pits and quarries, as well as other transport duties. During the summer when production was at its highest, horses and carters were brought over from the other side of the Forth. They were accommodated at Charlestown in Stable Row, at Craig's End and at the Parkneuk collieries. The horses were often fed on potatoes from a potato boiler. This was cheaper than hay or oats. Horses were valuable animals: in 1846 the Earl bought 2 horses "for the coal wagons" from John Young of Dunfermline: a black horse Charlie for £26 and another Bob for £22. So the cost of a horse was roughly equal to a man's wages for a year.

Today those magnificent creatures have almost disappeared from the scene and one is lucky to catch sight of a heavy horse, though we were once totally dependent upon them.

GRANARY

This was a store for grain and oatmeal. There was a hoist in the front centre of the building. On top was a splendid bell. This was rung to summon the workers in the morning and at finishing time etc. The bell and its housing were removed c1930 when the lads of the village were ringing it for fun. However by this time the Hygienic Laundry had a steam hooter which served the same purpose. Many of the tenants of the Estate delivered grain to the Earl in lieu of rent and this arrangement seemed to work to mutual advantage. It is probably over a century since grain was stored in the granary.

With the departure of the oxen, and the increasing need to feed and clothe the workers, the SUTLERY was established in 1804 in the ground floor of the building. Nearly 200 years later, the business still flourishes. Sometimes it has been run directly by the Estate with a manager, and at other times by a tenant.

With the limitations of transport as it was, the Sutlery, to all intents and purposes, had to provide everything that a family would require. Primarily naturally there were the staple diet items such as oatmeal, cheese, pease meal and butter. Most folks kept the odd pig in their yard as well as some hens and they also grew vegetables. Meat was also available from the Sutlery and 2 or 3 sheep were killed per week. Also, whenever animals were slaughtered for the big house, a proportion was sold on to the villagers at the Sutlery.

Granary and Sultery with School behind - note the Bell c1890

The Right Hon.ble The Earl of Elgin

Bot of James Bruce

1808   Dunfermline

April 4th   one hhd best malt aqua No 374
             65 Gallons @ 12/ ——————— £39 " "
             one bark rum No 269. 17½ Gal
             @ 16/6 ——————————— 14 . 8 . 9
                                              £ 53 . 8 . 9

             hhd bask if not returned 25/
             small do —— do —— 6/

             Settled in full this date
             as p Stamp receipt apart   Alexr Fairly
                                         p James Bruce

4 - 4 - 1808

Bill for barrel of whisky 1808

There was also a great deal of tobacco and snuff sold. Masses of lozenges, peppermints and liquorice were purchased ... this was probably necessary to clear the tubes of dust from the kilns. If the quantity of whisky sold in the sutlery is divided by the number of male workers, it works out at about 6 ½ bottles /man /week. This 'bottle a day' may be an overestimate as the ladies maybe had the odd sup also. However it is certain that the workers drank huge quantities of whisky to help to cope with the heavy work and kill the taste of the lime. The whisky was the finest single malt (at this time blending had not yet arrived) and in 1808 it cost 12/- (60p) per gallon. It arrived at the sutlery in a 65 gallon barrel. The price works out at 1/6 (7 ½p) per pint bottle. This may appear to be very cheap but, in the context of the wages at that time, it was relatively expensive. It does seem though that whisky was considered to be a necessity and not a luxury, and could account for ½ a man's wages.

Those items already mentioned were the big sellers but there were also goods you would expect e.g. tea, raisins, castor-oil, candles, soap etc. What was unexpected was the range and quality of items, especially of clothing. There was workers' clothing available but also good quality shoes, gloves, umbrellas and watches. In 1824 30 silk hats were sold. The village customers obviously bought good quality merchandise and the records of the sutlery prove it. The yearly takings of the sutlery were enormous: apart from the inn, there was really no alternative place to spend one's money.

In due course the Post-office was added to the business and it is still there. As we come to the 20th century, the range of items stocked decreased. It was possible to travel to specialist traders in Dunfermline to shop. It must be a long time since a silk hat or a gallon of malt whisky was sold in the sutlery. For quite a time the emporium was run by James Baxter and his daughters. His cheeses were a speciality taste - probably because he kept them next to the paraffin! He used to have daily encounters with a great-dane. This huge dog could swallow a half-loaf of bread whole, chased by Mr Baxter brandishing his butcher's cleaver.

The Sutlery has really been at the centre of village life since its conception. It has proved to be a vital integral part of the community and, with the closing of the laundry, is now the place where folks meet and gossip is exchanged.

THE QUEENS HALL

The Dunfermline Saturday Press & West of Fife Advertiser of Sat 16th 1887 carried accounts of events of the previous Sat under the heading "JUBILEE CELEBRATIONS AT BROOMHALL" Those activities were to mark the 50th year of Queen Victoria's reign at which the Dowager Countess of Elgin and Lady Louisa Bruce presented the Queens Hall to the villagers.

"Saturday the 9th July 1887, ought to be long remembered by the villagers of Limekilns and Charlestown - by the older members of the community as well as by the rising generation - as being one of the most important and interesting days in their history. Both villages were "en fete" on the occasion of the Queen's Jubilee. But it was no ordinary celebration. Due to the kindness of the Broomhall family, who have always manifested a lively interest in the people residing in their neighbourhood, there was handed over to the inhabitants of Limekilns and Charlestown a handsome suite of buildings, consisting of hall, reading room and library with a bowling green attached. In connection with the opening of the Village Club, as the institution is to be called, there was an appropriate ceremony, which was graced by the presence of the Earl and Countess of Elgin and other members of the family. The generosity did not stop here, however; for nearly two thousand people, including between three and four hundred Sabbath School children, were admitted to the grounds and liberally entertained".

The Hall is situated at the middle of the "C". It was designed to hold 300 people in the main hall, with recreation room, kitchen, committee room, toilets and kitchen attached. The cost of the complex was £1200. The regulations for the club were simple and it was open to all folks living in the vicinity. Cost of membership was set at 1d per week.

The article concluded "While a home has thus been provided for mental culture, it is satisfactory to notice that the Elgin family and villagers of the district have been quite alive to the necessity for healthy and invigorating outside recreation. Advancing with the times, the villagers are to have the opportunity of spending an hour with their favourite authors, and afterwards adjourn to the pleasant bowling green which has been turfed and opened near the club. The green is one of the finest in Fife, and ere long we anticipate that the Charlestown Bowling Club will take an important place among the clubs in West Fifeshire".

The village club survived until 1935 when the running of the hall became the remit of the Queens Hall Committee. This group have members from each user organisation and has successfully operated since it was formed. Something over 20 clubs and organisations consider the hall as their home. The hall is used for concerts, weddings, bazaars, meetings, jumble-sales, dances, lectures, church-services, polling days and parties. i.e. all varieties of public and private functions.

The library was discontinued c1980, but that apart, all of the aims and regulations stated over a century ago still operate and have stood the test of time. To this day, the Queens Hall still serves many of the cultural and social needs of the villages.

A NICHT WI' BURNS.

AN ENTERTAINMENT WILL BE GIVEN IN

THE QUEEN'S HALL, CHARLESTOWN,

On the Evening of FRIDAY, *the 25th January, 1889.*

Rev. J. G. CRAWFORD in the Chair.

PROGRAMME.

PART SONG	"There was a lad"	CHOIR
SONG	"Gae bring tac me a pint o' wine"	Mr J. DAWSON
SONG	"Afton Water"	Miss J. REID
RECITATION	"Halloween"	Mr J. ADDISON
SONG	"Last May a braw wooer"	Miss L. ANDERSON
QUARTETTE	"Here awa, there awa"	Misses J. REID, M. HUTCHISON, & M. ADDISON, & Messrs J. DAWSON & J. PATERSON.
SONG	"Braw, braw lads"	Miss M. BLACK
READING	"The posie, &c"	Mr A. WATSON
SONG	"My Nannie's awa"	Mr J. PATERSON
RECITATION	"Epistle to a young friend"	Mr J. KERR
SONG	"O whistle and I'll come to you, my lad"	Miss I. PITBLADO
RECITATION	"To a mouse"	Mr J. ADDISON

Interval of Five Minutes.

PART SONG	"Dainty Davie"	CHOIR
SONG	"Corn Rigs"	Mr D. HATELY
READING	"Epistle to J. Lapraik"	Mr J. ADDISON
SONG	"The weary pund o' tow"	Mr J. DAWSON
QUARTETTE	"Aye waukin, O"	Misses J. REID, M. HUTCHISON, & M. ADDISON, & Messrs J. DAWSON & J. PATERSON.
SONG	"John Anderson my Jo"	Miss J. REID
RECITATION	"Verses left in a rev. friend's house"	Mr J. ADDISON
SONG	"Scots wha hae"	Mr J. PATERSON
PART SONG	"Given grow the rashes"	CHOIR
RECITATION	"Tam o' Shanter"	Mr J. ADDISON

Finale, - - - "Auld Langsyne."

Admission, - - - Front Seats, 1s; Back Seats, 6d; under Twelve years of age, Half-price.

Tickets to be had from Messrs WILSON & MOODIE and A. FRASER, Charlestown; and Messrs W. JOHNSTONE and R. PURVIS, Limekilns.

Doors Open at 7.15; Chair to be taken at 7.45.

LIMEKILNS VILLAGE

A history of Charlestown would not be complete without a short look at our near neighbours. Charlestown and Limekilns are always thought of collectively as "the villages" with only the big brae between the two.

The name implies that lime was burned on a small scale at Limekilns from way back in time. The kilns were probably small and temporary since signs of only one remain. There is a rubble stone structure behind Main Street which was almost certainly a malt kiln.

There has been a harbour at Limekilns for centuries and the place contains quite a few places of note. ROSYTH CHURCHYARD dates back to the 12th century and some of the walls of the original church remain. There are gravestones dated early 17th century and many seamen are buried there. In the early 1800's, Burke and Hare rowed across the Forth and snatched bodies for sale to the University. A strong vault was built to put a stop to this practice.

In those times over 100 mastermariners came from Limekilns. There were around 4 barques, 17 brigs, 35 schooners, 32 sloops and a tug. Those sailed all over the globe. Some were built at BRUCEHAVEN SHIP YARD. Repairs were also done there and the yard closed c1900.

The most interesting archaeological feature of the village is the KINGS CELLAR. It was constructed for the monks of Dunfermline Abbey c1360. Wine for the Abbey was stored there and there is the belief that there exists a secret underground passage between the two. It probably also stored wine for the Kings at the Palace, hence the name. The building is in Academy Square and has been renovated many times. There have been quite a few uses and at present it is used as a Freemason's Hall.

The feudal superiors of most of Limekilns were the Halketts of Pitfirrane. A map of 1770 shows a large house there, Halketts Hall. This was likely to have been the summer residence and gives its name to this part of Limekilns. The centre of Limekilns had been bought by the Bruces c1589 from the Pitcairns. In 1815, the Earl of Elgin acquired the other pieces of the village from Sir Charles Halkett and so completed his ownership.

The church in the village was built in 1824 and serves the 3 villages: Charlestown, Limekilns and Pattiesmuir. There was a soap works at Capernaum and Elgin Ale was brewed at Brucehaven.

In 1912 there were 22 shops in Limekilns. Many of those were run by ladies, some of whom were widows. This is another insight into life at this time. There were 2 licensed grocers, 2 butchers, 3 grocers, 1 barber's shop, 1 wool shop, 1 cycle shop, 2 sweet shops, 2 newsagents, 2 post-offices, 1 baker, 1 tearoom, 2 chip-shops and 2 general stores. There was also a pub, a cafe and a hotel. Modern shopping methods have reduced this to a ¼ of what it once was.

Today there are many clubs and organisations and they all serve both villages. There has always been a healthy rivalry between the residents. This shows in such things as sporting events. Although Limekilns has double the population of Charlestown, they have yet to win the Tug-of-War at the annual gala!

Queens Hall

Train from Shipbreaking

CHAPTER FOUR

OTHER INDUSTRIES

MILLS ON THE LYNE BURN

It is indisputable that there have been mills powered by the water of the Lyne burn for centuries. This is the stream that flows through Pittencrieff Glen and reaches the Forth just west of Charlestown. The mills were situated over the last ½ mile or so from Pitliver as the burn winds down to the Forth. It may seem odd that 6 or 7 mills could exist and be viable on this stretch of what is really only quite a small stream. Each mill had its own dam and lade and they would have taken turns of the water... perhaps one or two days milling per week.

Working in from the Forth, the 1654 map (The Sherifdome of Fyfe), shows Iron Mill, Marks Mill, Wakemil, Foodymill, Ingemil (where Midmill is now) and Pitliver. Spelling has changed over the years but those were still to be found on a map of 1878.

Feddes Mill

The oldest Mill was Foothies Mill (Foodis, Foody).

This Mill was owned by the monks of Culross in the 15th century. Four generations of Fethys held the mill for nearly a century until 1611. However the mill takes its name from an earlier tenant Gilbert Fod and should be Foddis Mill. Fife speech has led to the change over the years in the same way as Crummy has become Crombie. Grain was ground there until early in the 19th century when it was rebuilt by a Frenchman in 1815 and became a snuff mill. This building stood on the bend of the main road beside the bridge over the burn and was demolished in 1969 when the A985 was improved at the junction.

NETHER MILL (MARKS) was a fulling mill as was WAULK MILL from 1550. Fulling was the name given to the process of cleaning and thickening cloth. Mills changed use over the years and Waulkmill became the centre of the spinning industry in the district. It finished as a Sawmill. The saw bench has been preserved on the Estate and may well be the oldest piece of industrial equipment remaining here. The impressive Waulkmill House which stands nearby what was once part of Pitliver Estate, but in 1815 it was let on a 999 year lease to Lord Elgin.

MERRYHILL FARM (MARYHILL) can be seen here with its distinctive silage tower.

MIDMILL was built in 1815. It was originally a thread mill and around 40 women worked there. It was turned into a grain mill, with an associated pig farm, by the Lumsden family. The last working water wheel on the burn operated until 1969 when a lorry with its tip up destroyed the overhead water channel. The 3 storey mill has been carefully converted to a private house but the water wheel is still in place.

There is uncertainty about how IRON MILL BAY took its name. There is a view that it came from the iron-works (foundry), but it is probable that it comes from the iron, as opposed to the wooden, mill wheel. Prior to this it was originally known as WHALEHAVEN, as whales used to bask here before the river became industrialised with an increase in shipping activities. Iron Mill Bay, until the building of Crombie Armament Depot before World War I, swept from Charlestown harbour to Kinniny point. The area where now the depot lies was Kinniny Braes.

No doubt there was iron work done at Iron Mill for many years but this is not well documented. What is not in doubt is that it was established by Earl Thomas as a FOUNDRY in 1795. It was run directly by the estate for decades. Pig iron was found in quantity in the mining on the Estate and from this local ironstone were made many items for the railway, the ships, the pits and the works as well as for export. For example, the ship's anchors made there were famous. A bill of 1847 for railway equipment shows wagon wheels, bushes, shafts, rails, chairs for rails etc. Some of those castings were heavy e.g. a wagon wheel weighed about 2 cwts (100Kg). The foundry was connected to the harbour by a canal so that the heavier castings could be floated down to the harbour. This also helped to flush out the silt from the harbour. When the railway was re-aligned by N.B.R. c1870, the canal was filled in and a rail link was put into the foundry.

In 1816 foundry workers were paid a daily rate according to their skill. The day was long, from 7.00 a.m. until 6.00 p.m., 6 days a week. The rate for a day varied from 5/- (25p) to 2/4d (11p). They were paid every 3 months in cash by the factor. Those were relatively high wages in those days when labourers were earning approx 1/- and women 6d per day.

In 1870, the foundry was let to the Morton family and Andrew Morton became the tenant. The Morton family lived in the Foundry House (now Aberlyne) which was built by the Estate in 1875 at a cost of £1105 3 / 6d. By 1900 the foundry had become the largest employer in the area. The workers arriving by train could alight at Shillinghill Halt which later also served the depot. The Mortons ran the foundry until it closed in 1937. The site and ruins of the buildings are clearly recognisable by the 2 towers. One tower housed the turning lathe and the other the "blower" for the retorts. There is a pleasant walk along the burn, past the BORE WELL and up the bluebell brae to exit at Merryhill farm.

The first record of the lands of PITLIVER is in the 10th century when it was granted by King Malcolm 1st and Queen Margaret to the Monastry at Dunfermline. The first mention of a mill was in a grant by the Monastry to Robert Richardson in 1563. So there must have been milling there for centuries. There is no sign of a mill today but it is most likely to have been a grain mill because of the associated farmland on Pitliver Estate. As will be evident, however, some of the mills changed in type over the years. The Wellwood family owned Pitliver Estate for centuries and it was sold to the Earl of Elgin in 1921. There have been quite a few changes since then. In this little corner of Fife can be seen the versatility of water power. Man's ingenuity has shown how a small burn was harnessed to be applied to grain, iron, snuff, fulling, thread and wood.

BRICKWORKS

Charlestown Brick and Tile Co. was founded c1780. This was one of the industries to spring up around the village. There have actually been 2 brickworks. The first was located on the road down to the foundry and was served by a branch off the wagonway. There are no signs of this works today.

Fireclay was found around the seams of coal pits and lime quarries. This had often to be removed before the lime and coal could be reached. So this was another example of using materials at hand and puting them to good use. Fire bricks were always required at the kilns. The intense heat meant that the bricks had to be replaced and the kiln relined: sometimes at the end of each season. There was also a small trade in fireclay with the Baltic countries.

The Government of the day gave grants for drainage and this gave rise to a big demand for drainage tiles. This was met by the brickworks and many farms around purchased and laid field drains from there. The first ones made were only 2" wide which was too small, and the drains were virtually useless. The diameter was increased and the drains were successful. The method was to grind down the clay and then squeeze it through a nossle. A steam engine was used to power this. It was then cut into 2ft lengths and dried in open-sided sheds.

The Estate paid the wages of the workers and a wage sheet of 1846 shows this. Workers were paid by the day; the rate determined by their skill. This was approx. 1/10 (9p) for full-time employees. There are listed a number employed for shorter periods at 6d per day. Those were probably labourers and boys who moved round the various works as required. One Alan McCrouther was paid the handsome sum of 4/2 (21p) per day... presumably he was the manager or foreman. It is likely that the men were also paid a bonus, depending upon how many bricks were produced.

The fire-clay from the mines ran out in early 19th century and a new brickworks was built on the Estate. This is located about ½ mile West of Broomhall House. The buildings are still there and the clay hole next to it is now the "brickworks pond". This is now used by the curlers of Broomhall Curling Club when it freezes to sufficient depth and a bonspiel can take place.

CHARLESTOWN
Brick and Tile Work,

T HIS Establishment is now in full operation, and have for Sale

Common Brick of every description.
Fire   do.   do.
Drain, House, and Ridge Tile,
At Moderate Prices.

The Common Clay from which the above are manufactured is very fine, and the Fire Clay proved to be of very superior quality.

The Works are situated close to the Harbour of Charlestown, a port well known in the Frith of Forth for its extensive Shipments of *Lime and Coal,* so that parties at a distance can have Cargoes made up with the various articles on the most advantageous terms, and at the lowest rates of freight.

Bricks, common, per 1000, . . . 30s
House Tiles, per do. 45s
Drain Tiles, per do. No. 1.—15 inches
    long. 3½ in. deep, 3½ in. wide, . 30s
Soles for ditto, ... 15s
Drain Tiles, per do. No. 2.—15 inches
    long 5½ in. deep, and 5 in. wide, 60s
Soles for ditto, ... 30s
Chimney Cans, each, from 1s 4d to . 4s 6d
Common Flower Pots, per doz. . 2s 6d
Moulded ditto, with flats, ... 7s 6d
Sea-kale Covers, each, ... 2s 6d
Water Pipes, 2 inches to 12 inches
    diameter, from 6d per yard, to . . 3s
Glazed Flues for inside of Vents, from
    9d per foot, to 1s 2d
Brown Pottery-ware, at moderate prices.

1st August 1840.

SHIPBREAKING AT CHARLESTOWN

ALLOA SHIPBREAKING CO.

Shipbreaking

By the turn of the century Charlestown could not compete with the deeper and larger ports such as Methil, Grangemouth and Bo'ness. There was a decline in the amount of commercial activity. However, at the end of the first world war, another chance happening was to give the harbour another lease of life and extend its life by around ½ a century.

This company was the creation of Robert Watson McCrone and was founded by him in 1922. It was to grow as Metal Industries into the largest shipbreaker in Great Britain and later expand into a huge industrial group. McCrone had been trained as an engineer in Edinburgh and after service in the war, he determined to start his own company. He was ambitious and efficient and persuaded Dr John Donald Pollock and Steven Hardie to join him with sufficient capital to buy ships for scrapping. Pollock was Chairman and front man with contacts to secure contracts: Hardie was vice-chairman and looked after the finances and McCrone as managing-director ran the business side. Those three Scots were to lay the foundations of a string of successful companies of which they could be justifiably proud. This empire was of course to make their personal fortunes.

McCrone had originally intended to use Alloa docks but the town council changed their minds and McCrone turned to Charlestown. The harbour was now being run by London & North Eastern Railway Co. after amalgamation of the railways. Agreement was reached to the benefit of the new company, though L.N.E.R. had the contract to deliver the scrap metal produced. Thus no ships were ever broken up at Alloa. The first to be treated at Charlestown was a

"Von Der Tann"

Naval sloop Hibiscus of 1250 tons. Charlestown harbour being tidal had some advantage for the breakers since a ship could be beached and the keel reached.

In Nov 1918 Admiral Sir David Beatty arranged for the surrender of the German High Seas Fleet. The ships were first sent to the Forth and then onward to Scapa Flow; but they were to return later under different circumstances. The fate of those warships was preempted by the German crews when they opened the seacocks of every ship and the whole lot went to the bottom. There were around 15 battlewagons and 25 destroyers. This was to prove to be good fortune for the new shipbreakers. By the time the Co. was becoming established, Ernest Cox was having some success in raising the vessels. His method was to have divers make the hulk airtight and then to pump it full of compressed air. The first few were destroyers, purchased by McCrone and broken up at Charlestown.

The larger battle-wagons had usually turned-turtle and had to be towed down to the Forth upside down. Those were too large for the harbour and so part of Rosyth Dockyard was leased, including a dry-dock, for the purpose. This meant that the battleships could be coped with. The first purchased was a British one, H.M.S. Ajax of 23,000 tons. The pattern became established so that ships were worked at Rosyth and the hulk towed to Charlestown for completion. So many famous warships ended their days at Charlestown: H.M.S. Ajax, King George V and Colossus amongst them. Colossus was the first British dreadnaught to have upper deck armour against aerial attack. Large profits were made from the Scapa operation; some of the battle cruisers were Seydlitz, Kaiser, Hindenburg, Bayern and Konig Albert. The Hindenburg was the only one raised the right

"Grace Harwar being towed in"

way up and the last to be raised in 1938 was the Derfflinger. Many of the destroyers came to Charlestown.

By 1930 the Co. had expanded to become METAL INDUSTRIES Ltd. Most of the trade was with surplus warships and those had valuable salvage non-ferrous metals and armour... brass, lead, bronze and copper. Merchant ships were, however, not neglected and the most famous of those was the Mauretania broken at Rosyth in 1935. An interesting vessel broken up at Charlestown was the Grace Harwar. She was a Finnish sailing ship... the first metal sailing ship built on the Clyde and the last to broken at Charlestown in 1935.

So what was happening to the Harbour whilst all of this was going on? The East ballast bank was a hive of shipbreaker's apparatus. There were cranes with concrete foundations, cutting equipment, an oxygen shed and railway lines all over the place. Much of the damage to the harbour walls dates from this period with heavy warships banging about.

McCrone himself had for many years a suite at the Elgin Hotel. He married Enid Just in 1934 at the age of 41 and purchased Pitliver Estate and House ½ mile North of the village. He resigned as Chairman in 1955 and lived on at Pitliver with his farms at Waulkmill until his death aged 89 in 1982. The Pitliver Estate has changed hands a few times since then. Charlestown over this period had been largely busy with ships less than 3000 tons. There were

Shipbreaking in the 1960's

naval destroyers, frigates, minesweepers and submarines. Towards the end of the operation many trawlers were broken up but the last one, in 1963, was a submarine H.M.S. Scorcher. In 1962 M.I. decided to close down at Charlestown due to lack of suitable vessels for sale.

Work had to be done to clear the site of all shipbreaker's equipment. The yard was returned to the British Transport Commission in 1963 and in due course to Broomhall Estate once the railway people had finished with it. Most of the 30 or so local workers were either paid redundancy or found employment in the dockyard. So came to an end this chapter in the life of the harbour. Approximately 500 ships had been broken up for scrap between Charlestown and Rosyth.

Today the harbour houses only pleasure craft. The West ballast bank is covered with private housing as are much of the surrounds. What of the future?... what new prospect is there for further use of this once thriving port, which has had such a varied and interesting history and played a vital part in the industrial development of this area of Fife?

SALTWORKS

There has always been a demand for salt and it has been manufactured from evaporated sea water for centuries in Fife, at least from the 16th. The method is to pump sea water into a pan under which coal is burned. The coal used was very poor quality and this may be one of the reasons why we had saltpans in Charlestown... to use up the low-grade dross from the Elgin collieries.

The pans were located near Easter Cottage at the foot of the big brae and of course right on the river. There were a number of pans, buildings and a tall chimney. There were many saltworks in Fife and one was run in Limekilns by the Halketts. Those at Charlestown were more modern. The pans were made of iron plates from the Foundry. These had to be replaced from time to time. The process was fairly skilled and the salters had to ensure that the fire burned continuously night and day. This made the salt water evaporate slowly and so made salt of better quality. It also prevented the pans burning out too quickly. The ashes had to be raked, the brine stirred and the salt drawn. The panhouses were hot, steamy and unpleasant places to work. So the salters, often women, were uncomfortable and worked long shifts, including night-work, for poor wages.

To begin with the operators were the CHARLESTOWN PATENT SALT CO. They used about 10 tons of coal per week. This eventually became THE LEITH SALT CO. They were still using the buildings after the works closed in 1946.

CHARLESTOWN RAILWAY STATION was next to this site - it had closed in 1935. The whole of this area was cleared in 1969 and now there is a row of private houses on the Saltpans. Opposite no.s 8 and 9 sits Easter Cottage, looking much as it did 100 years ago.

Easter Cottage, c1920

CHAPTER FIVE

PEOPLE

MEDICAL PROVISION

There was no National provision for medical care at the time Charlestown was created. The Estate had however already cover for workers and their families and Charles extended this in 1760. He engaged a doctor for this purpose on a permanent basis and paid all medical bills. This continued right up to 1864.

A lot of the work around Charlestown, particularly at the quarries and kilns, was dangerous. Anyone seriously injured and who could not be treated locally, was sent to Edinburgh Royal Infirmary. Pensions were paid out to those suffering disablement as a result of an injury in the Earl's employment. A bill for surgeon John Gil shows the kind of fees charged:-

Reducing a fracture of the leg with attendance... £11/-(guinea) 17 visits to Berrylaw (a pit)... ½ crown a time... £2 2/6. There is also the log book: actually a school jotter, of the village mid-wife (the houdie). She dealt with the births. This lady had charges for delivering a child ranging from 1/- to 10/-. This was not related to the difficulty of the birth, but to the ability of the mother to pay! It is an interesting wee book which also records whether mum is married or not.

There were dreadful things about then. In 1854 an epidemic of cholera devastated the villages and many folks died. Regular unwelcome visitors were diphtheria, measles, diabetes, scarlet fever, whooping-cough, tuberculosis and bronchitis. There were no powerful drugs to combat those and they were often fatal. It is only within the last 50 years that they have been tamed. The sort of medicine available then were things like rhubarb pills, blue pills, castor oil, lead and opium pills.

The villagers paid into the Sickness Society which was " the Independent Order of Foresters". There are still a few members about today. A Dr. Stenhouse, and later his son, provided cover over a long period. In 1826 his bill to the Estate for the ½ year was £600.

Unlike most of Scotland, Charlestown had no recorded sickness resulting from crude sewage. This was largely thanks to Earl Thomas' rules of 1815 and the method of collection (see Honey Cart). There was actually a sewage works completed in 1877 from Dunfermline to Charlestown following the course of the Lyne burn. Actually this was frequently discharged into the burn and in fact still is! However this system did not serve Charlestown and the villages had to endure their own arrangements for another half century. Incidentally neither was there piped running water into the houses until the 20th century. It had to be carried in buckets from the nearest well. The 8th Earl died in 1863 and the Trustees carried out many changes to the way in which the Estate operated.

The factor's idea was that the Doctor be paid a salary of £150 and could take on private patients. The Charlestown and Limekilns Medical Association was formed.. They charged 3d a week contribution. This organisation collected the money and paid the doctor. By the end of the 19th century, there were many such schemes in operation nationally. Charlestown's original had begun 100 years before most of them and so once again we can claim to be a forerunner and model for others to follow. This arrangement lasted until 1947 when the National Health Service came along.

Today the villages still enjoy better health provision than most. There is a well-equipped surgery which also dispenses. This adds to the quality of life, and along with the atmosphere of the place, means that the residents can expect long and healthy lives.

CHARACTERS

No self-respecting community would be complete without having thrown up a few characters and worthies Charlestown has had its fair, share. One of them was the village poet. ANGUS McDONALD FORBES lived at 9 North Row. Recently I was given a small booklet of his works from his grand-daughter. This is one of them:-

Reminiscences of Early Life.

Ye scenes of my childhood, fraught with sweet recollection,
    To embitter the present compared with the past ;
How oft have I drained your sweet stores of reflection,
    To soothe the dull hours which their shadows have cast.

The aspirings of childhood and dreams of my youth
    Have vanished—they too are things of the past ;
My schoolmates—ah where ? can I answer in truth,
    For varied the sphere where their lot has been cast.

They have left their dear homes—those havens of pleasure—
    Twice dear to the heart since its hearth can't be passed ;
Where mothers oft sigh as they think on their treasure—
    Their dear darling boy—when there he sat last.

Some have crossed the wild waves to a far distant shore,
    Unaided, unfriended—but mark as they go,
Their fancy oft wanders to scenes they adore,
    More than nature and art can on them bestow.

Some sail o'er the waste of the fathomless deep—
    Endure hardships and dangers which we never know ;
But fond recollection o'er their memories sweep,
    To the homes and the hearts that loveth them so.

Some have left the quiet village surrounded with beauty,
    Where cheerfulness reigns to enliven the scene ;
To trace out their wanderings I feel it my duty,
    For bright were the days which our childhood hath been.

The concord of youth in love's sunny morning,
    Unfaded, untarnished, for ever remain ;
Though our bark hath been drifting, life's message performing,
    The heart has been anchor'd, as bound by a chain.

Bright scenes of my boyhood, ever dear recollection,
    Where friendships were formed, and infancy grew,
When sweet concourse did charm the abode of affection,
    The homes and the hearts that hath ever been true.

                                        Angus McD. Forbes.
CHARLESTOWN, March 1878.

DAVIE ELDER

The Elgin Railway passenger service ceased when the N.B.R. took it over. Then for around 50 years we had horse-buses. Davie Elder ran the first of those between Dunfermline and Charlestown. A time table of the 1880's shows 3 different operators on the route. The rail passenger service was reinstated on the reconstructed line in 1895. Horse-buses however continued and were eventually superseded by the motor-bus. Davie retired c1910 and was given employment as a carter on the Estate. He operated with a donkey and cart, kept in the corn-yard behind the laundry. For many years Davie and Nora the cuddy, were a familiar sight as they moved slowly around the village green en route for Broomhall.

The blacksmith's shop was part of the Estate Workshops complex. There horses were shod for 200 years and broken items were repaired. The last blacksmith was JAMES WILSON, the son of a Crombie blacksmith. He was a powerful man clad in a leather apron and once a month he would appear at the laundry to use the phone to order his supply of oxygen cylinders. His roar of "Wulson frae Chairlesstoon" could probably have been heard in Glasgow without the instrument. In the early 30's his 'hammerman' was a village lass Annie Spence. I am unsure of when the last horse of many thousands would have been shod, but the shop closed in the mid 1950's.

THOMAS BAMBURGH - Village Hermit

This fellow could be classified as a real hermit. He lived with mother in the 'blue hoose' opposite Fiddlershall. His mother was the widow of a seafaring man. At an early age Thomas wished to follow in his father's footsteps but his mother was determined that he would not. Since his wishes were not to be granted the lad secluded himself in the garret of the house and was not seen by anyone for 25 years! He was fed by his mother through a hole in the ceiling and though they were able to converse, her last sight of him was 15 years before her death. Then there was no one to look after him and it was decided that he should be taken to the workhouse in Dunfermline. This was accomplished with some difficulty by 3 burly policemen. His appearance was weird and untidy and he had peculiar habits, which caused no little comment. However he did settle down and lived on for many years in his new environment.

ELDER'S LIMEKILNS COACH.
Leaving Limekilns .... at 8.40 A.M. and 2.40 P.M.
Leaving Dunfermline ....at 10.50 A.M. and 6.15 P.M.

CLARKES LIMEKILNS COACH.
Leaving Limekilns at 8.45 A.M., 1 P.M., and 5 P.M. Leaving Old Inn, Kirkgate, at 10.50 A.M., 4 P.M., and 6.15 P.M.

CANT'S LIMEKILNS COACH.
From Limekilns daily, except Saturdays, at 1 and 5 P.M; and on Saturdays, at 2 and 7 P.M. From Blyth's Hotel, Dunfermline, daily, except Saturdays, at 4 and 7.30 P.M.; and on Saturdays, at 5 and 9.30 P.M.

REMEMBERING DAYS GONE BY

A fascinating interview with Mrs Elizabeth Hamilton, then aged 90, recalling her childhood:-

"I was born in the Double Row Charlestown in 1897 on the 12th December. In those days there was no water in any of the houses and it had to be brought from various wells throughout the village. Each householder had a key with which they could draw the water as required and it was usually carried back in two pails at a time. As a young girl, to help my mother, I used to carry this water for her, often from as far as 6 houses away. I would then fill up the boiler and zinc bath so that she might be prepared for Tuesday morning's wash. Early on a Tuesday I would rise to find that my mother had already lit the boiler and was scrubbing the clothes on the board. Next she would put them into the large cast-iron boiler until any stains had been removed. Finally she would put the clothes out to dry.

During the Summer months the whitewashed clothes would be laid on the green to bleach in the sun. When they dried, my mother would go out with the watering-can and soak them so that they would become even whiter. From start to finish it took a long time to do the family's weekly wash. I often wonder what my mother would say were she to come back and see all the new gadgets on the market today.

When I was a girl, several men in the village were employed at Charlestown Foundry and it was the custom for the oldest child at school to take their father's or brother's, breakfast and dinner to the Foundry a mile away. As a child it was my turn to do this - to get up, get the breakfast and run down (usually in bare feet) with the two pitchers, one with tea and the other with food in it. In the winter time we had to go to the blacksmith's shop where Mr Wilson had a large round iron plate ready hot for us to put the pitchers on to heat up the tea again. While we waited to take the pitchers home again we would thaw out our feet in a warm lade nearby or play hide-and-seek among the wooden patterns that the moulders used. After that we took the empty pitchers home, then off to school. After our dinner, it was off to the foundry again with our father's dinner, but this time we did not have to wait for the pitchers. We went straight back to school. Sometimes one or two of the boys would take a shortcut through the farmer's field. One day the farmer, Mr Easson, caught them and he told them they had to go straight back across the field and then round by the road and that they were never to do that again. They had to run all the way back to school because if they were late they would get the strap! Those days have left me with happy memories.

When I was a girl I can remember Lord Elgin's grandfather and grandmother who were very good to the old people of the village. New Year's Day was a special day when the cook made a huge pot of hare soup for the old people. In the morning one of the Estate workers brought down a large barrow which was left at the lodge gates. The old people had to take a pitcher with their name tied to the handle, and this was put in the barrow. Then the barrow was wheeled up to the big house where the pitchers were filled with soup and they were collected again from the lodge gates. It was grand hare soup.

I look back on the day when I carried old Jean Struth's pitcher along to her house in the Double Row. She was a good old lady and I often went to sit beside her and listen to her stories. I was about 7 or 8 at the time. She had no carpet on her floor, just the old 7 inch square bricks and she had them scrubbed really clean. At the fireplace there was a small hearth rug, which she had made out of the rags and the kerb was made out of ½ a cartwheel. Her baffies were made of sackcloth and woollen rags, which she had made herself.

When I went over on Sunday she was sitting on her stool wearing a long white apron and her bible and white handkerchief were lying on the windowsill. She taught me many things, such as how to tell the time, how to see the back of my new dress using two mirrors and she told me one day that if you visit someone and another person comes in, you should always go first-never try to sit the other person out!

I remember when she asked me to go with her to the beach to gather "cracklans". I asked what they were "Oh" she said, "come with me". She rolled up a small sack and tucked it under her arm. She knew exactly where to go to find the cracklans, which turned out to be small pieces of coal washed in by the tide. They were clean and shining and made a grand fire. We filled her sack which she put on her back and made our way home up the Pan Brae, one of the paths which were used before the houses were built in East Harbour Road.

Jean's memory later deteriorated and she was finally taken to Cupar, where she died when I was fourteen. But I still have happy memories."

HARESOUP

This yearly arrangement arose from the tenants HARE DRIVE. All of the farmland was covered to thin out the number of hares and protect the next year's crops. The hares were used to make hare soup for distribution to the older villagers.

1891 CENSUS

Towards the end of the 19th century, transport systems had improved and the lime, coal and harbour trade had decreased. There had been a change in the type and place of work. The census of 1891 lists Charlestown, Limekilns and Pattiesmuir together.

OCCUPATIONS:

PROFESSIONAL

Teachers	7	+4 pupil-teachers
Music teacher	1	
Governess	1	
Pupils	318	
Solicitor	1	+2 apprentices
Customs Officers	2	
Minister	1	
G.P.	1	
Nurse	2	
Private means	22	/362

Most of those are self-explanatory... what about the last entry?

TRANSPORT

LAND

Railwaymen	9
Carter	9
Bus Driver	1
Coach Proprietor	1
Cab Owner	1

The bus was clearly the Dunfermline/Charlestown horse-bus.

SEA

Harbour	3	
River Pilot	7	
Shipping Agent	4	
Seamen	29	/64

INDUSTRY

Linen/damask	100	Young ladies now working in linen mills.
Iron making	63	Charlestown Foundry
Factory	13	
Mechanics	17	
Coal	11	
Boatbuilder	1	

Limestone quarry	4	
Stonebreaker	2	
General labourer	30	/251

FARMING

Farmers	6	
Agric. workers	81	
Landowner/Peer	1	/88
Domestic Service	88	This has virtually vanished today.

SERVICES

Dressmaking	25	Includes Tailors and Seamstresses.
Laundry	3	
"Keeps a mangle"	1	An interesting occupation.
Clerk	8	
Insurance	1	
Hotel/Pub	8	
Coal Merchant	1	
Gas worker	2	
Water	1	
Police	1	
Shop Assistant	36	/175

TRADE/CRAFT

Miller	1	
Baker	6	
Mason	3	
Slater	4	
Joiner	10	includes ship-carpenters.
Watchmaker	1	
Blacksmith	6	
Shoemaker	1	/32
Out of Work	4	Unemployment was low.
Paupers	7	/11

POPULATION

	Charlestown	Limekilns	Total
Male	247	299	546
Female	305	403	708
	552	702	1254

SIZE OF FAMILY

Children	0	1	2	3	4	5	6	7	8	9	10	11	12
No.	12	12	29	27	26	23	17	9	6	4	1		01/167

This gives an average number of children per family of almost 4.

AGE OF MARRIAGE

Age	No	Married	% Married
0-5	189		
6-10	178		
11-15	196		
16~20	131	2	1.5
21-25	92	11	12
26-30	94	43	47
31-35	69	45	65
36-40	72	57	79
41-45	83	71	86
46-50	74	63	85
51-55	42	34	80
56-61	51	47	92
61-65	38	35	92
66-70	34	33	97
71-75	35	30	85
76-80	17	16	94
81-85	12	10	83
86-90	4	4	100

This will show the expected Victorian pattern. Folks married later in life and stayed married. They had larger families than those of today. Those who wished had jobs of work which probably were for life. In the villages the social changes which have occurred over the 19th century are evident as are those in the century since then. The population in Limekilns and Charlestown today is much the same as 100 years ago but there are around double the number of houses/families and the number of children has reduced very much.

Yearly distribution by Estate to widows and retired workers from the big house.

CHARLESTOWN 24th JANUARY 1894.

Received this day from the Dowager Countess of Elgin:
6lbs tea, 10/- for sugar and parcel of clothing.
Distributed as follows:
Widow Joseph Wilson -Hood, ½ lb tea, 3lbs sugar.
Widow Alex McGregor -Hood, ½ lb tea, 3lbs sugar.
Widow John May -Hood, ½ lb tea, pair kneecaps, 4lbs sugar.
Widow Robert Addison - knitted shawl Widow Wm Roxburgh, knitted shawl, ½ lb tea, 3lbs sugar.
Widow James Calder - knitted shawl, ½ lb tea, 4lbs sugar.
Widow Alex Reddie - Hood, ½ lb tea, 3lbs sugar.
Widow John Roxburgh, ¼ lb tea, 3lbs sugar.
Widow Robert Hugh, ¼ lb tea, 3lbs sugar.
Jane Simpson - knitted shawl, ½ lb tea, 5lbs sugar.
Ann Henderson - 1 pair stockings, ½ lb tea, 4lbs sugar.
Janet Thomson - 1 pair stockings, ¼ lb tea, 3lbs sugar.
May Paterson- skirt, ¼ lb tea, 3lbs sugar.
Jean Izatt - 2 belts, ¼ lb tea, 3lbs sugar.
Maggie Dick - ½ lb tea, 5lbs sugar.
Mary Meldrum - ¼ lb tea, 4lbs sugar.
Jane Wishart - 1 pr boots.
Mrs Alex Wilson - 1 pr kneecaps.
Andrew Meldrum - 1 white shirt and gravat.
Henry Edward - 1 shirt, 3lbs sugar
Widow Thos Wilson - bolster.
Nelly Morrison - 1 flannel dressing gown

"Paddle Steamer at Aberdour"

SOCIAL ASPECTS

We have seen the housing provided, the early educational system, the medical care available, the treatment of sewage, the laundry for cleaning clothes and the facilities for social activities.

The treatment of workers had been abominable. Prior to 1775 in Scotland, miners, quarriers and salters were literally slaves of both sexes to the owner. The children were bound for life to the employer by the payment of arles at baptism. The relevant laws were relaxed by the end of the 18th century and an Act gave them freedom.

For long enough, the remuneration of workers was also very poor. We have already looked at some examples -there are many. A mason's pay in 1794 was 8d (3p)/day and in 1845 it was 2/- (10p) per day in Winter and 2/6 in Summer. Labourers were paid 1/2 (6p) the day at this time and beef was 3d per lb, butter 11 d / lb, cheese 3d / lb and a hen or duck cost 1 The master of a brig earned £6 per month. There was however full employment and there was no need for local folk to seek work elsewhere.

For many years, as previously recorded, letters had been carried by the post bringing orders to the works etc. Men had been employed as 'letter carriers'. For many years Davie Wilson was a carrier between the collieries and the harbour office. An important social innovation was the arrival of the PENNY POST in 1840. There was no telephone and this brought universal communication to all. The post and telegraph office later stood at the foot of the run, next to the harbour.

It has been claimed that drinking and producing children were the main relaxation of the men. Generally the men, and some women, were hard drinkers. The whisky produced commercially was 70% strength (it is now 40%) and single malt... so there were compensations for the hard work.

Many years later a set of assorted pots was discovered in the cellar of the Elgin Hotel. It was the practice for the factor, the gamekeeper, the doctor and the innkeeper to meet and mix the standard dram for the bar. Alongside was a copious supply of bottles of prune juice used as the colouring agent!

Many of the chores of the housewives - see Mrs Hamilton's memories - have now disappeared e.g. going for water, setting and emptying coal fires, blackening the range of ovens, whitening the doorstep, washing and bleaching clothes, scrubbing floors etc.

Socially Scotland was a primitive country in the 17th century. To an extent the progression of Charlestown from this state will be mirrored elsewhere in the land. However, as this story has unfolded, it should be clear that this progress started earlier in Charlestown than in the rest of the land. We can argue that Charlestown was at the forefront of reform and a model for others to follow.

Allan the baker's at Lochaber

Programme of Soiree.

PARAPHRASE II. ....TUNE—"Evan."

O God of Bethel! by whose hand
Thy people still are fed ;
Who through this weary pilgrimage
Hast all our fathers led :

Our vows, our pray'rs, we now present
Before thy throne of grace :
God of our fathers ! be the God
Of their succeeding race.

Through each perplexing path of life
Our wand'ring footsteps guide ;
Give us each day our daily bread,
And raiment fit provide.

O spread thy cov'ring wings around,
Till all our wand'rings cease.
And at our Father's lov'd abode
Our souls arrive in peace.

PRAYER.   SERVICE OF TEA.

ANTHEM .... " Rejoice in the Lord," ....CHOIR.

ADDRESS BY THE CHAIRMAN.

ANTHEM.............."Thine, O Lord, is the Greatness."...............CHOIR.

ADDRESS—REV. J. G. CRAWFORD.

HYMN 234.

Abide with me ! fast falls the even-tide ;
The darkness deepens ; Lord with me abide !
When other helpers fail, and comforts flee,
Help of the helpless, O abide with me !

Swift to its close ebbs out life's little day ;
Earth's joys grow dim, its glories pass away ;
Change and decay in all around I see :
O Thou who changest not, abide with me !

I need Thy presence every passing hour,
What but Thy grace can foil the tempter's power !
Who like Thyself my guide and stay can be !
Through cloud and sunshine, O abide with me !

I fear no foe, with Thee at hand to bless ;
Ills have no weight, and tears no bitterness :
Where is death's sting ? where, grave, thy victory !
I triumph still, if thou abide with me.

ADDRESS—REV. JOHN YOUNG, M.A.

ANTHEM.................................... " Peace be Still," ....CHOIR.

Service of Fruit.   Interval of Five Minutes.

ADDRESS—REV. DAVID RUSSELL.

10TH SCRIPTURE SENTENCE. PSALM cxxii. ver. 6–7.

" Pray for the peace of Jerusalem : they shall prosper that love thee. Peace be within thy walls, and prosperity within thy palaces."

ADDRESS—REV. DR. JOSEPH BROWN.

ANTHEM............."How beautiful upon the mountains,".........CHOIR.

ADDRESS—REV. J. W. DUNBAR, M.A.

PSALM XC., 16–17...TUNE—"Dunfermline."

O let thy work and pow'r appear
Thy servants' face before ;
And shew unto their children dear
Thy glory evermore :

And let the beauty of the Lord
Our God be us upon :
Our handy-works establish thou,
Establish them each one.

BENEDICTION.

Printed by A. ROMANES, at the "Saturday Press" Office, Dunfermline.

SUMMARY

Charlestown is thought of as a model village. Did it achieve the ideas of its creator - an ideal society in minature in which the inhabitants could enjoy employment, education and social stature? Perhaps the reader can now answer that question.

Nowadays there are no children chattering on their way to school; the granary is empty; the blacksmith's shop has disappeared; the bleaching green is now a private house; there is not a horse in sight; the bell is silent as is the laundry hooter; the harbour houses only private yachts; the sutlery hasn't sold a silk hat in years; the air is clean and free from the kiln smoke; private cars have taken over from the horse-bus; the mills on the burn are no more but the Lyne is still full of sewage and the Elgin Railway Station is now a tennis court; but as you walk along North Row there is still the feeling that Davie and Nora will appear round the green and that the honey cart is just around the corner. The people who live here know that this is a special place and that there has always been the feeling that the community is bound together as a sort of family, sharing experiences.

All of the industry has gone but it is rewarding to look for the signs that Charlestown was once the hub of a remarkable enterprise. The mixture of industry, agriculture and family life was unique and it is doubtful if there was anything like it anywhere in Scotland.

Kilns and Harbour today

SOURCES AND ACKNOWLEDGEMENTS

Author	Title	Publisher	Date
Aldridge & Tuxworth	Lord Elgin's Works	S.D.A.	1990
Buxton lan	Metal Industries	World Ship Society	1992
Chalmers Peter	Historical and Statistical Account of Dunfermline	Blackwood & Sons	1844
Chesher, Foster & Hogben	A Short History of Villages	Local Community Council	1979
McNaughton Douglas	The Elgin or Charlestown Railway	Carnegie Dunfermline Trust	1986
Reid Alan	Limekilns and Charlestown	A. Romanes	1903
Simpson George M. (Captain)	Fifty Three Years at Sea		
Smoult T.C.	The Landowner and the Planned Village 1730-1830		
S.W.R.I.	A Village History		1968
Westwood John	That Portion of Scotland	Herbert MacPherson	1948
Wingate Michael	Small Scale Lime Burning	Intermediate Technology Publications	1985

My personal gratitude is also due to my good friend Lawrence Hogben who researched much of the material: to the late Bill Spence who collected so many of the wonderful photographs, presented to us by his son Michael: to the Pitcairns for the census information and to Pat Gibbons of the Scottish Lime Centre.

WEIGHTS AND MEASURES

This study throughout uses IMPERIAL UNITS. The following conversions to Metric may be useful.

Length

1 inch	= 2.54 centimetres	
1 foot	= 12 inches	= 30.48 centimetres
1 yard	= 36 inches	= 0.9144 metre
1 mile	= 1760 yards	= 1.6093 kilometres

Weight

1 ounce	= 437.5 grains	= 28.35 grams
1 pound	= 16 ounces	= 0.4536 kilograms
1 stone	= 14 pounds	= 6.35 kilograms
1 ton	= 2240 pounds	= 1.016 tonnes

Area

1 sq foot	= 144 sq inches	= 0.0929 sq metre
1 sq yard	= 9 sq feet	= 0.8361 sq metre
1 acre	= 4840 sq yards	= 4046.9 sq metres

Capacity

1 cu yard	= 27 cu feet	= 0.7646 cu metres
1 pint	= 4 gills	= 0.5683 litre
1 gallon	= 8 pints	= 4.5461 litres

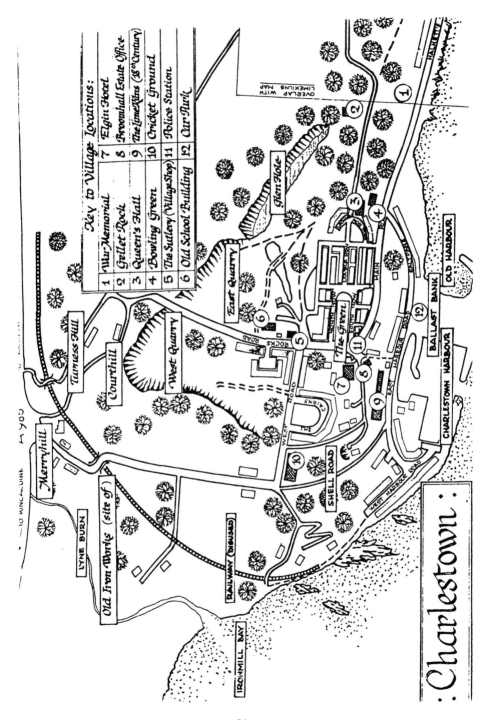

: Charlestown :

Key to Village Locations:

1	War Memorial	7	Elgin Hotel
2	Gellet Rock	8	Broomhall Estate Office
3	Queen's Hall	9	The Lime Kilns (18th Century)
4	Bowling Green	10	Cricket Ground
5	The Sutlery (Village Shop)	11	Police Station
6	Old School Building	12	Car Park

OVERLAP WITH LIMEKILNS MAP

HALKETTE

EAST HARBOUR ROAD

OLD HARBOUR

BALLAST BANK

CHARLESTOWN HARBOUR

WEST HARBOUR ROAD

SHELL ROAD

THE CAIRNS

WEST ROAD

ROCKS ROAD

MAIN STREET

SOUTH ROW

The Green

Glen Hole

East Quarry

West Quarry

Courthill

Furness Hall

Merryhill

LYNE BURN

Old Iron Works (site of)

RAILWAY (DISUSED)

IRONMILL BAY

10 KINCARDINE

TO ROSYTH

L 907

Charlestown

Lime Heritage Trust

Patron Earl of Elgin & Kincardine KT

NORMAN FOTHERINGHAM

Mr Fotheringham is a native of Charlestown where his family were proprietors of the Laundry from 1898 until 1970.

Upon graduating from Edinburqh University he served as a Lieutenant in the Royal Navy for five years. He returned to the village and assisted in running the family business until it was overtaken by washing machines in the home. He then served as a teacher in Dunfermline High School where he was Head of Mathematics for 25 years.

He is founder Chairman of the Gellet Society... the local history society and is now managing the CHARLESTOWN LIME HERITAGE TRUST which has been set up to tell the Charlestown Story.

Trust Director Norman Fotheringham B.Sc, BA.

c/o Scottish Lime Centre
Charlestown Workshops, Rocks Road, Charlestown, Fife KY11 3EN
T: 01383 872722
E: info@scotlime.org
W: www.scotlime.org